© Villiers Steyn/iStockphoto.com

Enrichment Magazine

IN THIS ISSUE . . .

Jesus the Storyteller 2

Parables in the Gospels 5

Shepherds and Sheep 7

The Kingdom of Heaven (and of God) 10

Marriage at the Time of Jesus 13

Literary Forms in the Gospels 16

A Denarius a Day 19

Samaria and Samaritans 23

Tax Collectors and Pharisees 26

Word Pictures 29

© iStockphoto.com

To the Director

This student folder contains nine study leaflets and the enrichment magazine. Distribute the leaflets as indicated in the leaders guide. This magazine should be distributed at the first session for use throughout the course.

3558 S. Jefferson Ave., St. Louis, MO 63118-3968
1-800-325-3040 • cph.org

Written by Cameron MacKenzie

Edited by Brian Chisamore

Cover art: *The Parable of the Two Sons* © Concordia Publishing House/Leslie Benson

Graphic design by Christina Ensign

This publication may be available in Braille, in large print, or on cassette tape for the visually impaired. Please allow 8 to 12 weeks for delivery. Write to Lutheran Braille Workers, P.O. Box 5000, Yucaipa, CA 92399; call toll-free 1-800-925-6092; or visit the Web site: lbwloveworks.org.

Manufactured in the United States of America

2 3 4 5 6 7 8 9 10 11 34 33 32 31 30 29 28 27 26 25

Jesus the Storyteller

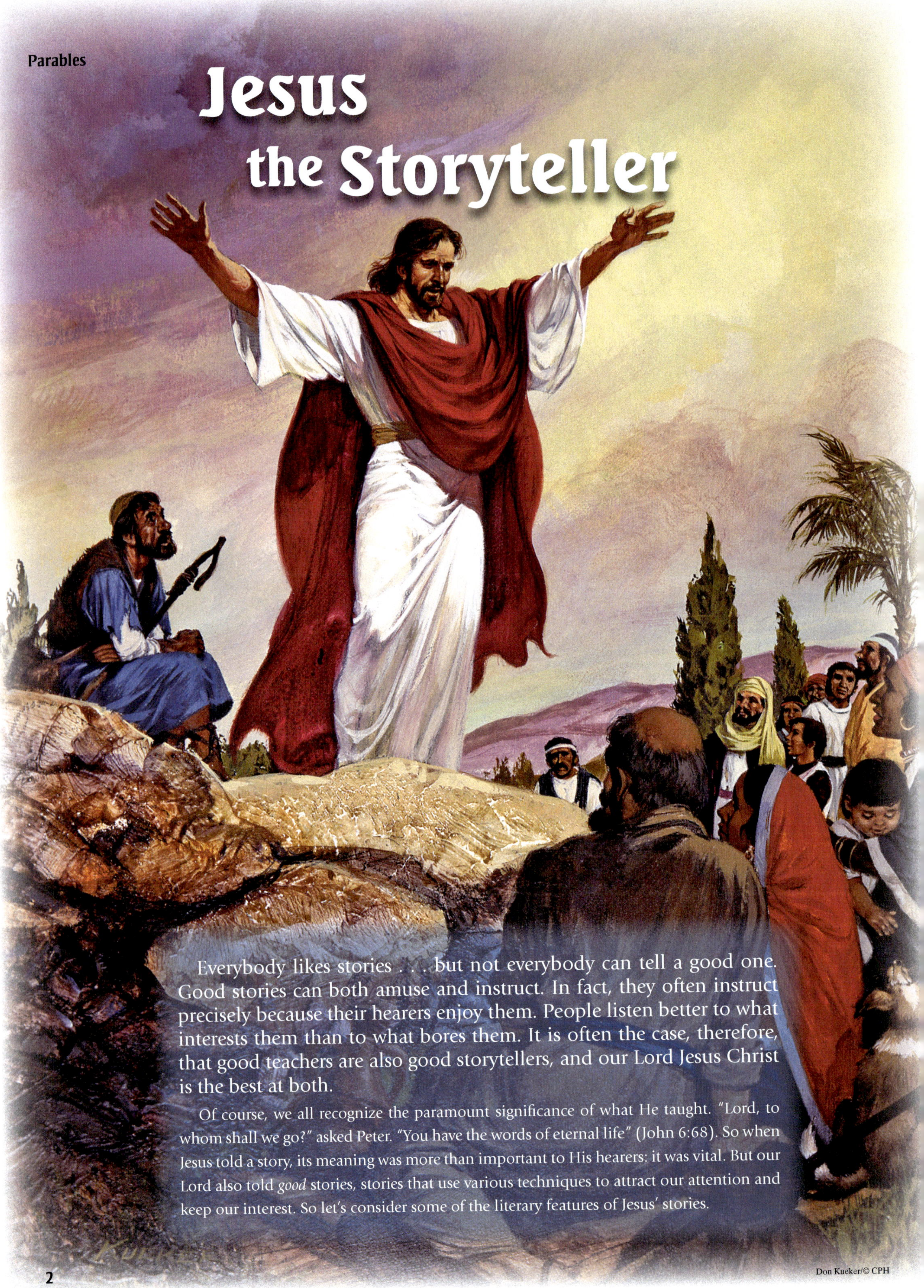

Everybody likes stories . . . but not everybody can tell a good one. Good stories can both amuse and instruct. In fact, they often instruct precisely because their hearers enjoy them. People listen better to what interests them than to what bores them. It is often the case, therefore, that good teachers are also good storytellers, and our Lord Jesus Christ is the best at both.

Of course, we all recognize the paramount significance of what He taught. "Lord, to whom shall we go?" asked Peter. "You have the words of eternal life" (John 6:68). So when Jesus told a story, its meaning was more than important to His hearers: it was vital. But our Lord also told *good* stories, stories that use various techniques to attract our attention and keep our interest. So let's consider some of the literary features of Jesus' stories.

Don Kueker/© CPH

Robert Hook/© CPH

Plots and Characters

Probably the first thing anybody might notice about Jesus' stories is their length. They are short stories—*very* short stories. Some, like the parable of the leaven (Matthew 13:33) are only one verse long; and even the longest of them, such as the parable of the prodigal son (Luke 15:11–32), do not even cover a whole chapter. Such brevity necessitates focusing on the main point and assists the hearer in remembering the story, but it also puts great demands on the storyteller. How do you make a story interesting when you are using so few words?

One thing that Jesus did was to make use of ordinary, everyday things familiar to His first hearers. You and I may not know much about first-century farming, vine dressing, or the Samaritans, but Jesus' first hearers certainly did. So Jesus could assume a great deal without having to spell it out. Or, to put it another way, Jesus' audience brought with them a host of experiences that helped them to understand what He was talking about. By using what was familiar, our Lord could make His point with a minimal number of words.

But there's always more to a parable than a connection to daily life. Most of us like stories that permit us in some way to escape the ordinary, not just repeat it—and Jesus' stories certainly do that. Perhaps you remember this explanation from your Sunday School days: "A parable is an earthly story with a heavenly meaning." This description certainly encourages us to look for a spiritual lesson in each story that Jesus told, but it is also a little misleading in that many of the stories are not "earthly" in the sense of "true to life." Often, they include details that are quite extraordinary, as if to show us that truths about God and His relationship to humanity are too great for simple comparisons taken from everyday experiences.

Consider, for example, the Good Samaritan (Luke 10:30–37). Not only is it unusual to receive help from someone who is an enemy of one's people, but also look at how generous the Samaritan is to the wounded man! He pays his bill and even promises the innkeeper to pay more when he returns. That's *not* the way it is in ordinary life.

Similarly, is it typical for business owners to pay those who work just one hour the same wage as those who work all day (Matthew 20:1–16)? Or for a father whose son has abandoned home to wait for his return every day and then, when he shows up, run to him and greet him with a ring and kiss (Luke 15:11–32)? Or for a man who is giving a banquet to send servants into the highways and hedges and compel people to come in (Luke 14:16–24)? Details such as these surprise us and intrigue us—and encourage us to look for a "spiritual" meaning.

© iStockphoto.com

Another story technique, closely related to the use of surprise, is to place the main point at the end. Parables are simple stories that revolve around just one point of conflict, that is, an event or situation that demands a resolution in order for hearers to feel satisfied and to sense that the story is complete. For example, we want to know what happens to the seed a farmer plants in different kinds of ground, or whether anyone will help when a traveler lies wounded along the road, or who will come when a man sends out invitations to a banquet. We expect stories—even very short ones—to reach a conclusion that answers the question posed by the plot, and the parables do so, often in surprising ways and usually in the conclusion.

Thus, in the parable of the sower (Matthew 13:3–9), we wonder whether any of the seed will ever reproduce fruitfully. It does—right at the end. In the Good Samaritan (Luke 10:30–35), we want to know who will stop and help. Jesus tells us that it is the last of the passersby—and the least likely candidate—who eventually shows compassion to the wounded man. And in the story of the great banquet (Luke 14:16–24), we are curious as to how the host will fill the banquet hall, until we learn—finally—that he orders his servants to force veritable strangers to come in.

By solving the plot conflict right at the end, the storyteller retains our attention. By doing so in a way that reverses our normal expectations, we feel satisfied both intellectually (no loose ends) and emotionally (we liked it!).

Besides plot, stories also include characters; and in longer stories, readers often enjoy seeing how characters grow and change. But detailed character development is impossible in stories as short as parables. Instead, Jesus uses pure character types to populate His stories. Amidst all the first-century trappings, readers throughout the centuries have recognized the characters because they behave in ways that are timelessly familiar: a selfish son wants his inheritance ahead of time; religious leaders show themselves hypocrites when they pass by a wounded man; and tenants want to cheat their owner out of the rent. We may not know anything about inheritance laws, priests, Levites, or tenants' rights and obligations, but we know the characters. They are our friends, acquaintances, and neighbors—maybe even ourselves.

Liking to Learn

By using character types that are universal and plots that are engaging, our Lord crafted numerous parables in order to teach "the secrets of the kingdom of heaven" (Matthew 13:11). Even though they are extremely short, the parables nevertheless reveal Jesus as a master teacher. Of course, we read parables for what they tell us of God, man, salvation, and the like. But even as we do so, our Lord encourages us to learn our lessons by means of stories that interest and intrigue. Yet another sign of God's love for us in Jesus, these stories make learning not only a blessing but also a delight.

Parables in the Gospels

Perhaps one of the most difficult things about studying and understanding the parables of Jesus is keeping them all straight. He told so many of those stories! They can be hard to find when we are looking for them. (Which Gospel account was it in again?) Some of them are repeated in the different Gospels. And there are even parables that seem similar to each other but turn out to be quite different. Since it can all get a little confusing, a table listing all of Jesus' parables can be a helpful tool.

Keeping Them Straight

The passages that are included in a table of parables depends on one's definition of a parable. The one employed here is the familiar one of a story—however brief—used by Jesus to teach a spiritual truth. This is meant to exclude parabolic *sayings* that our Lord also used frequently in His teaching, such as, "You are the salt of the earth" (Matthew 5:13) or "I am the good shepherd" (John 10:11). Opinions will differ as to whether such sayings should also be included in a chart that lists parables.

Another challenge to creating a table is what to call the individual parables. Many of them have long-standing, familiar names, and changing them to fit more contemporary terminology is more likely to confuse than to help. So we still list the parables of the sower and of the prodigal son. On the other hand, some traditional titles are likely to miscommunicate or perhaps not communicate at all to the modern reader. For example, we have renamed the parable of the "wicked husbandmen" to that of the "wicked tenants."

Finally, the chart here lists the parables by frequency of appearance—first those that appear in three of the Gospel accounts, then those in two of the Gospels, and finally those in only one. Again, opinions may differ as to whether parables such as that of the talents should be listed separately from that of the ten minas because they are very similar. Nevertheless, we have concluded that they are different enough in content and context to be classed as two separate stories rather than as two variations on just one.

A Blessed Purpose

Experiencing confusion or frustration in studying God's Word is a terrible thing, because it puts a barrier between us and some aspect of God's gracious workings on our behalf. And so, it keeps us from fully enjoying and giving thanks to Him for all of the benefits He gives to us in our Lord Jesus Christ.

May the table here aid you in your study and guide your heart and mind in plumbing the depths of the riches of the Gospel of Christ.

The Many Parables of Jesus

PARABLE	MATTHEW	MARK	LUKE
The Sower	13:3–9, 18–23	4:3–20	8:5–15
The Mustard Seed	13:31–32	4:30–32	13:18–19
The Wicked Tenants	21:33–44	12:1–9	20:9–16
The Leaven	13:33		13:20–21
The Lost Sheep	18:12–14		15:3–7
The Weeds	13:24–30, 36–43		
The Hidden Treasure	13:44		
The Pearl of Great Value	13:45–46		
The Net	13:47–50		
The Unforgiving Servant	18:21–35		
The Laborers in the Vineyard	20:1–16		
The Two Sons	21:28–32		
The Wedding Feast	22:1–14		
The Ten Virgins	25:1–13		
The Talents	25:14–30		
The Seed Growing		4:26–29	
The Two Debtors			7:40–48
The Good Samaritan			10:30–37
The Impudent Friend			11:5–10
The Rich Fool			12:16–21
The Barren Fig Tree			13:6–9
The Great Banquet			14:15–24
The Lost Coin			15:8–10
The Prodigal Son			15:11–32
The Dishonest Manager			16:1–13
The Rich Man and Lazarus			16:19–31
The Unworthy Servants			17:7–10
The Persistent Widow			18:1–8
The Pharisee and the Tax Collector			18:9–14
The Ten Minas			19:11–27

Shepherds and Sheep

It's probably going too far to say that you can't understand the Bible without knowing about shepherds and sheep, but such knowledge sure helps. From Genesis (4:2) to Revelation (22:3), the Bible is filled with references to shepherds and sheep—and lambs too. Sometimes the references are literal and other times figurative. Exodus 22:1, for example, describes the penalty for stealing sheep, but Psalm 80:1 prays to God as the "Shepherd of Israel."

One of the most endearing passages in the Bible begins with "The LORD is my Shepherd" (Psalm 23); and one of Jesus' most famous self-descriptions is that of the Good Shepherd (John 10:11). Both together have been the source of countless pictures and images. Then again, John the Baptist called Jesus "the Lamb of God" (John 1:29), and Christians ever since have used this title in hymns and liturgy to describe the Savior.

So learning about shepherds and sheep can deepen our understanding of the Bible.

Not an Easy Job

References to sheep in the Bible arise from the fact that raising such animals for their wool and meat was an important way for people to make a living in biblical times. Adam and Eve's second son, Abel, was a shepherd, as were the patriarchs mentioned later in Genesis. They were nomads. By taking advantage of broad tracts of uncultivated land, they provided for themselves and their families without investing much capital. Sheep multiplied naturally, and their food and drink were "free."

Some shepherds lived in villages, and their herds grazed on cultivated land after crops were harvested. During the worst weather, shepherds might also put their sheep into enclosures in order to protect them, but the ideal was not to feed them by hand in a pen but to get them out to good pasture.

Shepherding was not an easy life, and what the shepherd did not have to pay for in terms of food and water was more than made up for by hard work and a demanding lifestyle. In order to make the system work, the sheep had to be constantly moving to where good grazing was available; and they had to have men always close at hand to keep track of them.

This meant some real challenges for shepherds. First of all, they had to contend with the weather—everything from extreme heat to cold and wet—with nothing but temporary shelters such as tents and primitive clothing perhaps made from sheepskins or goat hair. These were serviceable, but hardly comfortable.

Then there were robbers and predators, including snakes, lions, and wolves. Shepherds would use weapons like wooden clubs (sometimes studded with metal) or slings to hurl stones against attackers. But they did not always win these fights, so faithful shepherds risked their lives for their sheep. Obviously, if the shepherds were careless or incompetent, the sheep were at risk. They depended on their shepherds.

Religious Significance

Besides satisfying economic purposes, sheep also played an important role in Old Testament religion as offerings sacrificed to God. There were different kinds of sacrifices, and each kind had its own purpose, specified by God Himself (see Leviticus 1–6). Rams were sometimes used for "burnt offerings" that had as their function access to God's favor. Rams also constituted the "guilt offering" for sins of desecration (unintentional or suspected) or sins of misusing God's name (for example, perjury). A layperson would offer a female sheep or goat as a "sin offering" for certain unintentional sins. The same animals were also sacrificed for some intentional sins. Sheep could also be used for the "peace [or fellowship] offering" that provided sacred meat for a meal that symbolized renewed fellowship with God.

In every instance, the sacrifice removed an obstacle of sin between the worshiper and God. However, as the Book of Hebrews reminds us, "It is impossible for the blood of bulls and goats"—and sheep too!—"to take away sins." Instead, such sacrifices were a "shadow of the good things to come instead of a true form of these realities" (Hebrews 10:1, 4). The real sacrifice for sin was, of course, Jesus Christ.

Perhaps the most familiar of the Old Testament sacrifices involving sheep was that of the Passover lamb. Instituted by God through Moses at the time of the exodus (Exodus 12:24), Passover was celebrated every year thereafter by faithful Israelites. They recalled the amazing story of God's deliverance of His people by the sacrifice of an unblemished lamb whose blood they had smeared on their doorposts to ward off the Angel of Death. However, the annual Passover celebrations not only pointed backward to what God had done for Israel but also forward to what He promised to do for all people in Christ.

In one of the best known of all Old Testament messianic prophecies—Isaiah 53—the Bible portrays the Savior as the Lamb of sacrifice. First, it describes people as "sheep": "All we like sheep have gone astray; we have turned—every one—to his own way" (v. 6). But then it adds that God has provided a substitute: "And the LORD has laid on Him the iniquity of us all. He was oppressed, and He was afflicted, yet He opened not His mouth; like a lamb that is led to the slaughter, and like a sheep that before its shearers is silent, so He opened not His mouth" (Isaiah 53:6–7).

John the Baptist immediately linked our Lord with such passages by designating Him "the Lamb of God, who takes away the sin of the world!" (John 1:29). It also was no accident that Jesus' death coincided with the Passover celebration and that, like the lamb, He was unblemished (by sin) and His bones were not broken (John 19:36). Paul therefore confessed, "Christ, our Passover lamb, has been sacrificed" (1 Corinthians 5:7).

Jesus—Both the Lamb and the Shepherd!

When the Bible was first written, probably most—if not all—of its original readers knew a lot about sheep and shepherds. So they realized at once what the Scriptures meant when they called God "the Shepherd of Israel" and Jesus Christ "the Lamb of God." For most of us today, such familiarity with the world of the Bible is impossible. We can *learn* about sheep and shepherds, but we cannot experience their world.

But it doesn't really matter. We may not know much about sheep, but we know a lot about being "lost." We may have never met a shepherd, but we understand what it means to need a protector. We may never have celebrated Passover, but we all need a Savior. And in our Lord Jesus Christ, we have exactly what we need. Precisely because He is "the Lamb of God who takes away the sin of the world," He is also our Good Shepherd.

The Kingdom of Heaven (and of God)

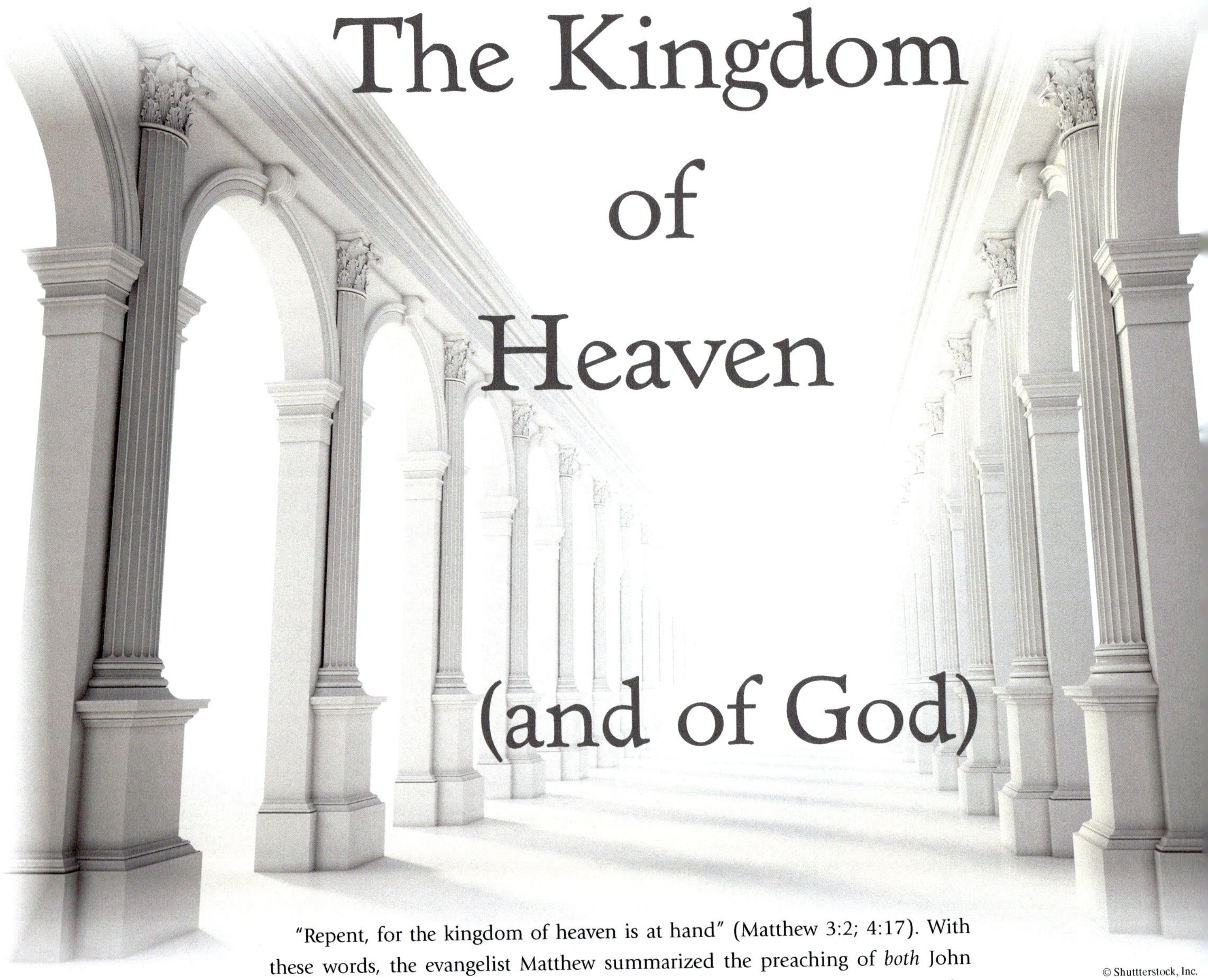

© Shuttterstock, Inc.

"Repent, for the kingdom of heaven is at hand" (Matthew 3:2; 4:17). With these words, the evangelist Matthew summarized the preaching of *both* John the Baptist and Jesus Christ at the beginning of their respective ministries. The "kingdom of heaven" or its equivalent, "the kingdom of God," is a central theme of New Testament Christianity, and in the Lord's Prayer, Jesus even instructed His disciples to pray for its coming.

Jesus also told His disciples that He used parables to reveal "the secrets of the kingdom of heaven" (Matthew 13:11), and He often began His parables with the phrase, "The kingdom of heaven is like . . ." This little phrase summarizes both what God did for humanity in Christ, the Savior, and what He still intends to do at the end of time.

The King and His Kingdom

First, let's consider a few statistics. The term "kingdom of heaven" is unique to the Gospel of Matthew, where it occurs thirty-two times. On five other occasions, the evangelist employed "kingdom of God." Luke used the latter expression thirty-two times, and Mark fourteen times. There are also two occurrences in

John (3:3, 5), as well as a few instances elsewhere in the New Testament. There are also passages in which the same idea occurs but is phrased differently or perhaps just shortened. An example of the former is the Second Petition, "*Thy kingdom* come" (see Matthew 6:10; Luke 11:2); an example of the latter occurs in Luke 12:31, "Seek *His kingdom,* and these things will be added to you." Obviously, "kingdom" terminology is worth studying.

But why did Matthew primarily use "kingdom of heaven," while Mark and Luke used "kingdom of God"? And are they really the same? The answer to the second question is, clearly, Yes. The two terms often occur in parallel passages; that is, accounts of the same incident in two or more of the Gospels. A good example is the parable of the mustard seed. Matthew (13:31) wrote about the "kingdom of heaven," whereas Mark (4:30) and Luke (13:18) referred to the "kingdom of God." But in Matthew 19:23–24, Jesus employed both phrases in such a way as to identify them: "only with difficulty will a rich person enter *the kingdom of heaven*. . . . It is easier for a camel to go through the eye of a needle than for a rich person to enter *the kingdom of God*" (emphasis added).

As to why Matthew used the term "kingdom of heaven" most of the time, we can only speculate, but perhaps he—like many pious Jews of the time—wished to avoid using the name of God if he did not have to, and since "heaven" is the place that defines God's presence and power, it was a nice substitute. The phrase also ties in with Jesus' teaching that His kingdom was "not of this world" (John 18:36).

Neither phrase appears in the Old Testament, but the concept has deep roots in the first part of the Bible. God is depicted as the "king" of His people in a few passages; for example, Zephaniah 3:15, "The King of Israel, the Lord, is in your midst; you shall never again fear evil." Sometimes also, He is depicted as the "king" of the entire world, such as in Psalm 24, "The earth is the Lord's and the fullness thereof. . . . Who is this King of glory? The Lord, strong and mighty, the Lord, mighty in battle!" (vv. 1, 8).

The Bible refers to the Lord's kingship both as a present reality (e.g., Psalm 145) and as a future occurrence (Isaiah 24:23; Obadiah 21). Moreover, it associates the future kingdom with a messianic deliverer. The familiar prophecy of Isaiah 9:6–7 is a good example: "For to us a child is born, to us a son is given; and the government shall be upon His shoulder. . . . Of the increase of His government and of peace there will be no end, on the throne of David and over His kingdom." Another occurs in Daniel 7:13–14, where the prophet describes One coming on the clouds, "like a son of man," and to Him is given "dominion and glory and a kingdom."

Accordingly, when John and Jesus began to proclaim the Kingdom, they were using a familiar idea. What was unfamiliar was their announcement that the kingdom was "at hand." In John's preaching, that meant it was imminent—very, very close—but in Jesus' preaching, it meant that the Kingdom had arrived! For Jesus was the King, and belonging to the Kingdom meant following Him. As the angel said to the Virgin Mary, "He will reign over the house of Jacob forever, and of His kingdom there will be no end" (Luke 1:33).

The terminology "kingdom of God" is multifaceted. In any particular passage, it can represent either the present or future activity of Christ in either judgment or blessing; and the disciples can be described as either possessing it already or waiting to enter it. In the Beatitudes, for example, Jesus described the "kingdom of heaven" as the present possession of "the poor in spirit" and of those who are persecuted for the sake of righteousness (Matthew 5:3, 10). Yet, He said that on Judgment Day, the King would invite those on His right to "inherit the kingdom prepared for you" (Matthew 25:34). In the present, God sustains us by His promises of forgiveness, resurrection, and life; and in the future, He will grant us final and permanent deliverance from all evil.

But in every instance—now and future—relationship to Jesus is the key. The Pharisees once asked Him when the Kingdom would arrive, and Jesus told them, "The kingdom of God is in the midst of you" (Luke 17:21). It was already here because Jesus was here. This is good news for those who follow Him—like being invited to a wedding feast—but for those who do not accept Him, it means "weeping and gnashing of teeth" (Matthew 22:2–3, 13).

Law and Gospel

The Bible clearly associates the kingdom of God with judgment. Because God is righteous, He will set all things *right*. Evil may flourish today, but divine judgment will surely come. This is a part of what we pray for when we say, "Thy kingdom come."

But it is not the whole story, for the Judge is also the Savior. Right now, He sustains us with His Word; but then, we shall experience the fulfillment of His promises. To believers, therefore, the kingdom of God is a concept of comfort. We belong to Him now and for all eternity because the Lord is our King.

Marriage at the Time of Jesus

Marriage has been a part of human history since creation. Right from the beginning, God made human beings male and female and united them in marriage. Jesus Himself affirmed this institution when he quoted Genesis 2:24, "Therefore a man shall leave his father and his mother and hold fast to his wife, and the two shall become one flesh," and then drew the conclusion, "What therefore God has joined together, let not man separate" (Matthew 19:5–6). For Christians, therefore, marriage is here to stay.

But marriage *customs* vary greatly. The ways people negotiate, enter, and commence married life differ with time, place, and people. Our Lord referred to marriage and the customs of His day when teaching His disciples. Of course, they didn't have to study the customs. They knew them by experience. But times do change. In order for us to comprehend more fully the message of the New Testament, we need to learn about marriage practices at the time of Jesus.

© iStockphoto.com

A Family Affair

Most people—then and now—get married. But how do they do it? How, in the first place, do they find a prospective spouse? To a considerable degree these days, individuals have to fend for themselves. Friends and family may help by suggestions and introductions, but courting, proposing, and becoming engaged are left to the man and woman themselves.

In biblical times, this was not the case. Marriage involved family and property, and it took place normally when the bride and groom were still in their teens. The first step was betrothal. This resulted from negotiations between a prospective groom and the father of an eligible female. The couple were probably not unknown to each other, and some sort of mutual attraction could already exist (although not necessarily). Think, for example, of Rachel and Jacob (Genesis 29:18). But the formal decision was that of the prospective bride's father, who would consider not only the personal qualifications of the young man involved but also his family and the bridal price. For the groom paid an amount of money—large or small, depending on circumstances—to the bride's family in order to marry her.

Once the negotiations were completed, the man (either in person or by his representative) and the woman exchanged vows before witnesses (Malachi 2:14). There could also be a written contract. Although this solemn pledge between the two was called the "betrothal," we should not confuse it with a modern-day engagement. The latter expresses an *intention* to get married; the former *constituted* the marriage. Even though the couple did not immediately start living together, they did not exchange any further vows and they could not break their betrothal upon any grounds other than those that would terminate a marriage.

A betrothal like this was the relationship that existed between Mary and Joseph at the time of Mary's pregnancy. The Bible calls her "wife" and him "husband," but they were not yet living together, so Mary's condition prompted Joseph to decide on a "divorce." At the intervention of an angel, however, Joseph did not carry through his first intention but instead took Mary into his home as his wife, because she was with child by the power of the Holy Spirit (Matthew 1:18–25).

From *Fear Not, Joseph!* / © CPH

Robert Hook/© CPH

At some point after the betrothal (maybe as much as a year later), the couple would start living together. During the interval, both individuals made final arrangements for commencing their new life together. Finally, the time would come, and family and friends would celebrate the wedding.

The celebration began with a procession by the groom and his attendants from his home to that of his father-in-law in order to get his wife. This usually took place at night, and the groom's arrival was heralded by a great shout. Our Lord made use of this custom in His parable of the ten virgins (Matthew 25:1–13). In the story, the uncertainty regarding the time of the groom's arrival turns into a long delay with dire consequences for the maidens who slept and so failed to replenish their lamps.

After reaching his wife's home, the groom, now accompanied by his bride, attendants, family, and friends proceeded to the couple's new home (perhaps only an apartment within the groom's father's place) and to the bridal chamber, where their life together would begin. On one occasion, John the Baptist described himself as "the friend of the bridegroom" and our Lord Himself as the groom (John 3:29).

Festivities could continue for as long as a week, but they began with a great feast in the couple's new home. Jesus and His disciples attended such a wedding feast, at which the Lord began His ministry of miracles by turning water into wine (John 2:1–11). On a later occasion, Jesus compared the kingdom of heaven to a wedding feast given by a king for his son (Matthew 22:1–14). Besides the refusal of the invited guests to come, this story describes another transgression of Jewish customs, the presence of a man without a "wedding garment" (v. 11). People expected one another to dress appropriately for such a joyful occasion.

Christ's Bride: The Church

The reference to a wedding feast as a likeness for God's kingdom perhaps hearkens back to the description of the messianic feast in Isaiah 25:6–9. Similarly, the notion of the Messiah as a heavenly bridegroom has roots in Old Testament imagery that likened God to the husband of Israel; for instance, "For your Maker is your husband—the Lord of hosts is His name" (Isaiah 54:5).

But the culmination of such metaphors occurs in Ephesians 5, in which the apostle Paul compares the love of Christ for His Church to that of a husband for his wife: "Husbands, love your wives, as Christ loved the church and gave Himself up for her, that He might sanctify her, having cleansed her by the washing of water with the word" (vv. 25–26). As Martin Luther often explained, Christ took from His Bride what was hers—all sin and unrighteousness—and gave her what was His—complete obedience and holiness. In this way by grace, our Lord Himself established the perfect marriage between Himself and His Church—neither contemporary nor traditional, but extraordinary and eternal.

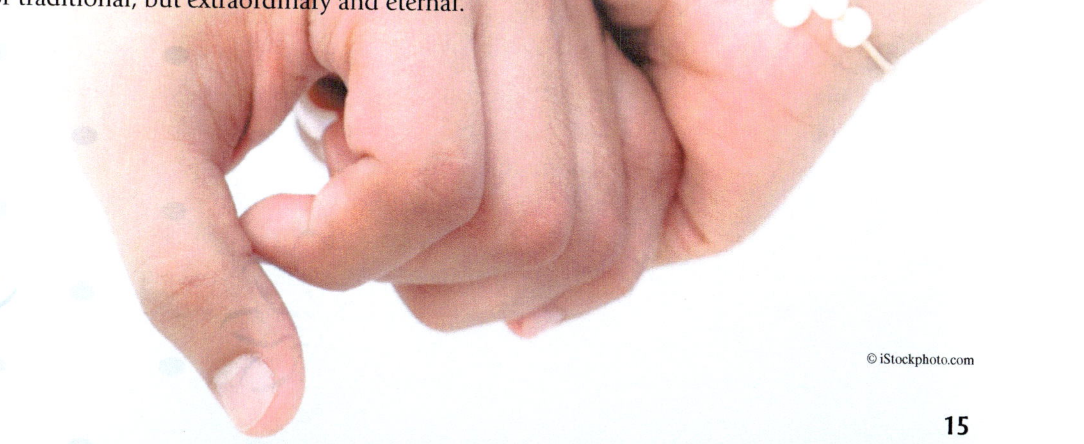

© iStockphoto.com

LITERARY FORMS IN THE GOSPELS

Most Bible readers realize that the writers of Scripture used different kinds of literature (or genres) in presenting God's Word. We find poetry in the Psalms, narratives in the Historical Books, and visionary literature in Daniel and Revelation. So, in order to get the most out of our Bibles, we should be familiar with the various "rules" that writers followed when using such forms. Psalm 23 makes the same point as 1 Peter 5:7, "He cares for you," but it does so by means of poetic word pictures instead of just prose. Differences in genre matter.

The most important genre for Christians is that of "Gospel." There are four of them in the Bible, and each presents a unique but complementary portrait of Jesus. In doing so, however, the writers of the Gospels made use of literary subtypes or subgenres on account of the various ways in which our Lord revealed Himself by word and deed. Parables, for example, are a literary form that Jesus used repeatedly in His teaching. But there are several others in the Gospels, and having some familiarity with them can reveal the literary merits of these books and—more importantly—illuminate their contents.

Words and Deeds

Elsewhere in this magazine, we have examined stories as one way in which our Lord instructed His followers. But stories were not the only way. The evangelists also record sayings, sermons, and dialogues, and each of them has its own characteristics.

By *sayings*, we mean those statements of Jesus that can stand alone as advice or doctrine. Often, the evangelist sketches a context (when, where, and to whom spoken) that originally gave rise to a saying. For example, a man once asked Jesus to settle an inheritance dispute, and our Lord responded, "Take care, and be on your guard against all covetousness, for one's life does not consist in the abundance of his possessions" (Luke 12:13–15). Another time, someone called out, "Blessed is the womb that bore You, and the breasts at which You nursed," to which Jesus answered, "Blessed rather are those who hear the Word of God and keep it!" (Luke 11:27–28). In both cases, Jesus' response is memorable and valuable even apart from its context.

19. Look over your answers to Questions 15–18. In light of them, what do these two parables mean: who purchased what and why?

Day 5 • Read Matthew 13:3–9, 18–23

THE PARABLE OF THE SOWER

20. Should a farmer worry about the soil conditions where he is planting seed? Why or why not?

21. Why do you think God isn't worried about the "soil conditions" where He is preaching His Word?

22. How are the parables examples of God spreading His Word almost recklessly?

23. *For personal reflection. Sharing optional.* What tribulations, persecutions, or cares of this world threaten to choke out the faith God has created in you through His Word?

12. The mustard seed is quite small, but it can grow to be larger than any other plant in a garden. How is the kingdom of God like a mustard seed?

13. Read Daniel 4:4–12, 19–22. What do the birds represent in the vision? (If it helps, lump the birds together with the wild beasts.)

14. In light of your answer to Question 13, what do the birds represent in the parable of the mustard seed? What does this say about the kingdom of God?

Day 4 • Read Matthew 13:44–46

THE PARABLES OF THE HIDDEN TREASURE AND THE PEARL OF GREAT VALUE

15. Read through the beginnings of the parables in Matthew 13. Who is the main actor in all the parables except the two in verses 44–46? What does that suggest about the main actor in these two parables?

16. Why does the man in the parable of the hidden treasure sell all he has to purchase the field with the hidden treasure? What does he hope to gain?

17. Why does the merchant in the parable of the pearl of great value sell all he has to purchase the pearl? Can he hope to make money on the transaction?

18. Who is God's treasured possession?

Deuteronomy 7:6

Deuteronomy 26:18

Malachi 3:16–18

What light might these verses shed on the parables of the hidden treasure and the pearl of great value?

Day 5 • Read Mark 2:22

NEW WINE IN OLD WINESKINS

19. New wine has been through one round of fermentation, but it continues to ferment if left to itself. What happens to wine as it ferments, and what is the by-product? (A little online research might help you here, or a conversation with a wine connoisseur.) Why would old wineskins burst if filled with new wine?

20. Read Jeremiah 31:31–34. Name two differences between the old covenant and the new covenant.

21. If the old wineskin in the parable stands for the old covenant, and if the old wine stands for fasting, then how is Jesus like new wine?

22. In a few sentences, explain what the three parables in Matthew 9:14–17 and Mark 2:18–22 say about why Jesus' disciples are not fasting like the disciples of John the Baptist and the Pharisees.

12. Why would people not fast while the bridegroom is with them? (Hint: When would the bridegroom be with a group of people?)

13. Who is the bridegroom Jesus mentions in Matthew 9:15? Based on your answer to this question and number 12, why were Jesus' disciples not fasting?

14. Who was fasting? What is different about Jesus that His disciples were not fasting?

Day 4 • Read Mark 2:21

A NEW PATCH ON AN OLD GARMENT

15. Why does no one use unshrunk cloth as a patch for clothing?

16. A key phrase in the parable may be "the new from the old." What is Jesus saying about Himself versus John the Baptist and the Pharisees?

17. Read 2 Samuel 12:14–23 and Ezra 8:21–23. How did people in the Old Testament use fasting?

18. If the disciples were to fast while Jesus was with them, it would be like sewing unshrunk cloth onto an old garment. How so?

19. Read Isaiah 58:1–7. (Note that God's words in v. 2 are somewhat ironic.) What about the people's fasting did God object to?

20. Why did the Pharisee in the parable not go home justified before God?

Day 5 • Read Luke 18:9–14

THE PARABLE OF THE PHARISEE AND THE TAX COLLECTOR

21. What was the tax collector's attitude toward God? Which actions or words described in the parable support your answer?

22. How is the tax collector's prayer different from that of the Pharisee?

23. Read Psalm 51. What sacrifice does God desire, according to the psalm?

24. How does the tax collector's prayer reflect the teachings of Psalm 51?

25. Why did the tax collector go home justified while the Pharisee did not?

Day 3 • Read Matthew 20:1–16

THE PARABLE OF THE LABORERS IN THE VINEYARD

11. Jesus uses the parable of the laborers in the vineyard as an illustration for what (see v. 1)?

12. Why do the workers hired first complain at the end of the day? Is their complaint justified by human standards? Is the owner's practice in line with typical human labor practices?

13. Because the parable is about the kingdom of heaven, what the workers hired first complain about must have a spiritual equivalent. What is the spiritual equivalent of their complaint? Do you know anyone who makes this kind of complaint?

14. Read Matthew 19:23–30. To whom does Jesus tell the parable of the laborers in the vineyard? To whom do you think He is responding? Why?

15. Because the parable is about the kingdom of heaven, what is Matthew 20:15 telling us about God's kingdom?

Day 4 • Read Luke 18:9–14

THE PARABLE OF THE PHARISEE AND THE TAX COLLECTOR

16. To whom does Jesus tell the parable of the Pharisee and the tax collector?

17. What works does the Pharisee talk about? Why does he list the works in his prayer?

18. Read Matthew 23:1–12, 23–28. Summarize in a few bullet points what Jesus says about the Pharisees.

18. After squandering his property, the younger son decided to go back to his father. What was his plan (vv. 18–19)? What is the difference between a son and a servant, and why would the son ask to be the latter?

19. Some of Jesus' contemporaries (and some people in our own day) might say the father was soft, even foolish toward his son in verses 22–24. What evidence can you see of such softness in the text?

20. Read verse 24 closely. Do you agree with the father that the son was lost and now is found? What difference does the answer to that question make? (Revisit your answer to Question 16.)

Day 5 • Read Luke 15:11–31

THE PARABLE OF THE PRODIGAL SON

21. Does the story feel complete in regard to the older son? Explain your answer.

22. What is the older brother's complaint about the celebration? How does it relate to the Pharisees' complaint in Luke 15:2?

23. The younger son asked to be treated like a servant. How was the older son acting? Find evidence in the text to support your answer.

24. Based on all you've learned so far, how did the Pharisees understand God and His love?

25. If the father in the story stands for God, then how is God different from the way the Pharisees understood the father?

10. What point is Jesus making to the Pharisees with this parable?

Day 3 • Read Luke 15:8–10

THE PARABLE OF THE LOST COIN

11. *For personal reflection. Sharing optional.* What would you think of a shepherd who loses his sheep? What would you think of a woman who loses 10 percent of her nest egg through utter carelessness?

12. Read Ezekiel 33:1–11. What does God do to or for sinners? Why?

13. Does the woman's invitation to her friends and neighbors in Luke 15:9 seem to fit the occasion of finding her lost coin? Explain your answer.

14. Based on your answer to Question 13, how much does God rejoice over one sinner who repents?

15. If God rejoices over a sinner who repents, what attitude should the Pharisees have?

Day 4 • Read Luke 15:11–31

THE PARABLE OF THE PRODIGAL SON

16. The previous two parables are named for the lost sheep and the lost coin. What do you think is a more fitting name for this story, "The Parable of the Lost Son" or "The Parable of the Prodigal Son"? Explain your answer.

17. Was the younger son ever going to be entitled to the share of the property that was coming to him? If so, when? What does that mean about his request?

19. Why is it significant that the judge does not fear God? Consider these verses:

Genesis 20:11

Genesis 22:12

Exodus 18:21

Leviticus 25:17

20. What finally moves the judge to listen to the woman?

Day 5 • Read Luke 18:1–8

THE PARABLE OF THE PERSISTENT WIDOW

21. a. What promise do these passages convey?

Psalm 135:14

Psalm 146:5–7

Isaiah 61:8

Romans 5:1–5

b. How is that promise communicated in the parable of the persistent widow?

22. How do these passages, along with the parable of the persistent widow, encourage you in prayer?

Hebrews 4:14–16

Romans 8:31–34

23. Open a copy of Luther's Small Catechism and look at the first two commandments and their meanings (or recite them from memory!). Why does loving, fearing, and trusting in God above all things lead us to call upon Him in prayer? How does the parable reinforce that point (see vv. 7–8)?

24. Does the parable mean that God will give us what we pray for if enough people are praying the same prayer at the same time or if one person repeats the same request often enough? Why or why not? (If you have trouble, look at vv. 6–7, and then ask which prayers Jesus is talking about here.)

25. *For personal reflection. Sharing optional.* Why pray?

Day 3 • Read John 15:1–8

THE VINE AND THE BRANCHES

11. What does it mean to abide in Jesus? How can we do that? See verse 7 for some help.

12. How do these passages reflect the message of Jesus' parable in John 15?

Romans 10:14–17

Colossians 3:16

1 Peter 1:22–25

1 John 1:1–4

13. What causes a grape branch to bear fruit? What causes a Christian to bear fruit in his or her life?

14. What practical steps can you take to abide in Christ? (Consider the Third Commandment, "Remember the Sabbath day by keeping it holy.")

15. Does the fruit you bear save you? Explain your answer (perhaps with help from your answer to Question 13).

Day 4 • Read Luke 18:1–8

THE PARABLE OF THE PERSISTENT WIDOW

16. Jesus helps us here by telling us what the parable of the persistent widow means. What is its point?

17. Jesus seems to compare God to an unjust judge. What problems does this raise? How might you resolve them?

18. Read Matthew 7:11. How does this passage help explain the parable of the persistent widow?

19. Read Exodus 22:7–15, 25–27 and Leviticus 19:9–17. Who is our neighbor, according to these verses?

20. Who were the Samaritans? (Use a Bible dictionary if you have one; otherwise, look up John 4:9 for a hint.)

Day 5 • Read Luke 10:25–37

THE PARABLE OF THE GOOD SAMARITAN

21. The priest and the Levite were going down from Jerusalem to Jericho, a town where many temple workers lived when they were not on duty. The road (which exists to this day) was notorious as a place for violent robberies; it had many places where bandits could hide. How might this explain the seemingly callous actions of the priest and the Levite?

22. Read Numbers 19:11–13, 20–22. How might this explain the actions of the priest and Levite? (Keep in mind that the priest and Levite were headed home after finishing temple duties.)

23. Read Deuteronomy 22:1–4. What does this passage require? Would it apply in any way to the case of a person lying half dead by the side of the road? Why or why not?

24. Read Matthew 12:9–14. How would the Pharisees answer Question 23? How about Jesus?

25. What risks did the Samaritan take by rescuing the man on the side of the road? What costs did he incur?

Day 3 • Read Luke 12:13–21

THE PARABLE OF THE RICH FOOL

11. Read Luke 12:22–34. How does this passage (which comes right after today's parable) help explain the meaning of the parable of the rich fool?

12. Look at verse 19; then look up Psalm 103:1–5. What is the problem with what the rich man says to himself?

13. Who will get the rich man's possessions after he dies? What difference does the answer make?

14. Read Psalm 14. Why does God call the rich man a fool in the parable?

15. What sin does the parable try to shake us out of? How does it prepare us to hear Jesus' words in verses 22–34?

Day 4 • Read Luke 10:25–37

THE PARABLE OF THE GOOD SAMARITAN

16. What is the setting for the Parable of the Good Samaritan (vv. 25–28)?

17. Lawyers in Jesus' day were men, typically Pharisees, who had studied the Old Testament laws very carefully and could apply them to specific cases. What evidence suggests that the lawyer knows he cannot earn eternal life?

18. Why might the lawyer have tried to justify himself after answering Jesus' question (v. 29)?

20. Some people claim that a loving God would not send people to hell. How would you respond on the basis of this parable?

Day 5 • Read Luke 13:6–9

THE PARABLE OF THE BARREN FIG TREE

21. What is the problem with the fig tree in this parable?

22. Read Luke 13:1–5 and Matthew 3:8. What do you think the fruit in the parable stands for?

23. What plan of action does the vinedresser suggest? Who might the vinedresser be, and why does he ask for more time? (See Romans 8:34 and 2 Peter 3:9 for a hint.)

24. What will happen to the fig tree if it does not bear fruit? What does that stand for?

25. Sometimes people hear the word "fruit" in these parables and believe it stands for good works, as if people who do good works will enter the kingdom of heaven. Read verses 2–3 and explain why that cannot be what Jesus means.

12. Read Jeremiah 20:2; and 37:15. Tradition says Isaiah was sawn in half by King Manasseh (see Hebrews 11:37). Who is represented by the servants in Matthew 21:34–36?

13. Whom do the tenants in the parable represent (v. 45)?

14. How are the chief priests and Pharisees like the tenants in the parable?

15. What will happen to the chief priests and Pharisees, and why?

Day 4 • Read Matthew 22:1–14

THE PARABLE OF THE WEDDING FEAST

16. Look at verses 6–7. How realistic do these actions seem? Explain your answer.

17. When a prince got married in the ancient world, the wedding was not simply a private affair. Why do you think that was? What message do the invited guests send when they do not show up to the marriage feast of the king's son?

18. Whom do the originally invited guests represent? How about those who were invited later (vv. 9–10)?

19. Read Isaiah 61, and then reread verse 10. Now read Revelation 7:9–17. What does the wedding garment in the parable stand for? What does it mean that one guest had no wedding garment and got thrown out of the wedding feast?

19. a. According to Matthew 12:48–50, to whom does the word "brother" (or "brothers") refer?

b. Now read Matthew 10:42. What light does this shed on the meaning of Matthew 25:40 and 45?

20. Does Jesus send the goats away because of their works (or lack thereof)?

Day 5 • Read Matthew 25:31–46

THE SHEEP AND THE GOATS

21. What does it mean in these verses to be blessed? Does it have to do with our works?

Matthew 5:3–11

Matthew 13:16–17

Matthew 16:17

22. How does your answer to Question 21 explain the meaning of Matthew 25:34?

23. For whom was the kingdom of God prepared, and when was it prepared? What comfort does this give you?

24. Are the righteous in this story invited to heaven because of their works? Explain your answer.

25. Read Titus 3:4–7; Romans 8:12–17; and Matthew 25:34. How did we become heirs? How do these three passages affect your answer to Question 24?

Day 3 • Read Matthew 25:14–30

THE PARABLE OF THE TALENTS

11. Read verses 24–25. What does the wicked servant say about his master? What does this imply about his view of God?

12. Read verses 20 and 22. How are the other two servants' words different from those of the third servant? What do their words imply about God?

13. Whose joy is referred to in these verses, and how does that joy affect us?

1 Chronicles 16:27

Nehemiah 8:9–12

14. What invitation do the first two servants receive (vv. 21 and 23)? How does your answer to Question 13 help explain this invitation?

15. According to the parable of the talents, are good works optional? Do our own good works save us? Explain your answer.

Day 4 • Read Matthew 25:31–46

THE SHEEP AND THE GOATS

16. Read Deuteronomy 27:15–26. Who gets cursed, and why? What light does this shed on Matthew 25:41?

17. For whom was the eternal fire prepared? Was it prepared for human beings? If not, why do some human beings end up there?

18. What works did the cursed omit in verses 42–43?

19. Read Luke 21:34–36 and Revelation 16:15. What does it mean to stay awake? (Look back at Session 7, Question 19 for help understanding the robes or garments.)

20. To whom was Jesus giving the Eschatological Discourse? Whom did He intend to hear His words, according to Mark 13:37?

Day 5 • Read Matthew 24:43–51

THE PARABLES OF THE MASTER AND THE THIEF AND THE TWO SERVANTS

21. If you always knew exactly when someone was going to steal from you, how would you respond? How would you act during times when you knew no one was going to steal from you?

22. *For personal reflection. Sharing optional.* If you knew exactly when Jesus was coming back, how might you be tempted to live in the meantime? (Be honest!)

23. How does the wicked servant in Matthew 24:45–51 live when he thinks the master will be away for a long time? What happens to him as a result?

24. Read 1 Thessalonians 5:1–11. How are Paul's words like the parables Jesus tells in Matthew 24:43–51?

25. What will happen to the servant who is acting faithfully when his master returns?

Day 3 • Read Matthew 24:36–41

JUDGMENT DAY

11. Who knows when Judgment Day will occur?

12. Jesus compares Judgment Day to the flood in the days of Noah. Who was swept away, or taken, in the days of Noah, and who was left? What does that imply about the people in Matthew 24:39–40: who gets taken, and who gets left?

13. What will people be doing on the day when Jesus comes back? Why?

14. Read 2 Peter 3:8–10. How do these verses support your answers to Questions 12 and 13?

15. Why would Jesus warn us that no one knows when He will return?

Day 4 • Read Mark 13:32–37

THE PARABLE OF THE DOORKEEPER

16. Jesus told this parable as part of the Eschatological Discourse (see Question 6), but it is not recorded in Matthew. How does it fit with what you read for yesterday?

17. Why would the master of the house order the doorkeeper to stay awake? You might consult a Bible dictionary if you wish to develop a deeper answer.

18. What is unbelievable about the master's orders in the parable? How are we like the doorkeeper in the parable?

3. What is odd about the bridegroom's actions and words in verses 10 and 12?

4. Read Revelation 19:6–10. What is the marriage feast in this and other parables?

5. How can we be ready like the wise virgins?

Day 2 • Read Matthew 24:32–35

THE PARABLE OF THE FIG TREE

6. Read Matthew 24:1–3. What is the initial occasion for the whole speech in Matthew 24 and 25? (This speech is called the Eschatological Discourse.) What are the two questions the disciples ask in 24:3?

7. Read Matthew 24:32–42. What is the point of verses 32–34? What is the point of verses 36–42? Are the two passages referring to the same event? Why or why not?

8. Matthew 24 and 25 answer the two questions posed by the disciples in 24:3. Try to identify in which verse Jesus moves from answering the first question to answering the second.

9. If the parable of the fig tree is talking about the end times, what is its message?

10. If the parable of the fig tree is talking about the destruction of the temple, then what is its message?

Watching for Eternity

Matthew 24:45–47

Distribute before session 9 for use in session 9.
Use enrichment magazine pp. 13–15.

Resources for Worship

Use these resources for your daily study at home and at the week's assembly.

Hymn

"Wake, awake, for night is flying,"
The watchmen on the heights are crying;
"Awake, Jerusalem, arise!"
Midnight hears the welcome voices
And at the thrilling cry rejoices:
"Oh, where are ye, ye virgins wise?
The Bridegroom comes, awake!
Your lamps with gladness take!
Alleluia!
With bridal care
Yourselves prepare
To meet the Bridegroom, who is near."

Zion hears the watchmen singing,
And all her heart with joy is springing;
She wakes, she rises from her gloom.
For her Lord comes down all-glorious,
The strong in grace, in truth victorious;
Her star is ris'n, her light is come.
Now come, Thou Blessèd One,
Lord Jesus, God's own Son,
Hail! Hosanna!
We enter all
The wedding hall
To eat the Supper at Thy call.

Now let all the heav'ns adore Thee,
Let saints and angels sing before Thee
With harp and cymbals' clearest tone.
Of one pearl each shining portal,
Where, joining with the choir immortal,
We gather round Thy radiant throne.
No eye has seen the light,
No ear has heard the might
Of Thy glory;
Therefore will we
Eternally
Sing hymns of praise and joy to Thee!
(*LSB* 516)

Prayer

Almighty and everlasting God, whose Son ushered in Your kingdom and opened it to all believers, keep me from falling into despair or apathy during these end times, and help me to remain ever ready for Your Son's return, that I may greet it with rejoicing, through Jesus Christ, my Savior. Amen.

Digging Deep
My Personal Study for Week 9

Day 1 • Read Matthew 25:1–13

THE PARABLE OF THE TEN VIRGINS

1. The virgins in this parable were probably accompanying the bridegroom for part of the procession before the marriage feast. What made the wise virgins wise and the foolish ones foolish?

2. We may find it rude or selfish for the wise virgins not to share their oil with the foolish ones. However, since this parable is really talking about being ready for Jesus' coming, what might their not sharing represent?

4. Why would Jesus wait until Judgment Day to separate believers from hypocrites in the visible church? (What could go wrong if He separated them earlier?)

5. What comfort do you draw from the fact that Jesus will not separate hypocrites from believers until the Last Day? From the fact that He *will* separate hypocrites from believers?

Day 2 • Read Matthew 13:47–50

THE PARABLE OF THE NET

6. If possible, use a Bible dictionary or online resource to learn about commercial fishing practices in Jesus' time. Write a few of your findings here.

7. For whom do the good fish stand? The bad fish?

8. Read Psalm 1 and Romans 4:1–8. What makes people righteous?

9. What is the place where there is weeping and gnashing of teeth?

Matthew 8:12

Matthew 22:13

Matthew 24:51

Luke 13:28

10. What comfort do you draw from the fact that God will judge the evil on the Last Day?

Looking for Judgment Day
Matthew 25:21

Distribute before session 8 for use in session 8.
Use enrichment magazine pp. 10–12.

Resources for Worship

Use these resources for your daily study at home and at the week's assembly.

Hymn

Rejoice, rejoice, believers,
And let your lights appear;
The evening is advancing,
And darker night is near.
The Bridegroom is arising
And soon is drawing nigh.
Up, pray and watch and wrestle;
At midnight comes the cry.

The watchers on the mountain
Proclaim the Bridegroom near;
Go forth as He approaches
With alleluias clear.
The marriage feast is waiting;
The gates wide open stand.
Arise, O heirs of glory;
The Bridegroom is at hand.

The saints, who here in patience
Their cross and suff'rings bore,
Shall live and reign forever
When sorrow is no more.
Around the throne of glory
The Lamb they shall behold;
In triumph cast before Him
Their diadems of gold.

Our hope and expectation,
O Jesus, now appear;
Arise, O Sun so longed for,
O'er this benighted sphere.
With hearts and hands uplifted,
We plead, O Lord, to see
The day of earth's redemption
That sets Your people free!
(*LSB* 515)

Prayer

Almighty and everlasting God, whose Son died that I may have life, turn open sinners to repentance, work faith in people who attend church for the wrong reasons, and preserve me in the faith, that all may hear our Savior's invitation to enter the kingdom prepared for us from the foundation of the world, through Jesus Christ, our Lord. Amen.

Digging Deep
My Personal Study for Week 8

Day 1 • Read Matthew 13:24–30, 36–43

THE PARABLE OF THE WEEDS

1. Read Matthew 7:21–23. What phenomenon is Jesus referring to in this passage? How does the parable of the weeds relate to this phenomenon?

2. Read 1 Corinthians 10:1–12 and Isaiah 29:13–16. How big a problem was hypocrisy in Old Testament times?

3. Read Acts 5:1–11 and Galatians 2:11–14. How big a problem was hypocrisy in the Early Church?

4. How does Abraham respond in verse 29? To whom is Jesus telling the parable (see v. 14)? What is Jesus implying about how they understand the laws of Moses?

5. Explain Abraham's statement in verse 31.

Day 2 • Read Matthew 21:28–32

THE PARABLE OF THE TWO SONS

6. To whom is Jesus telling the parable of the two sons (v. 23)? To which son do they correspond?

7. What makes the tax collectors and prostitutes like the first son?

8. What is the will of our heavenly Father, according to verse 32? What did John the Baptist say that the tax collectors and prostitutes believed but the chief priests and elders did not?

9. Read Deuteronomy 18:15–19. Who fulfilled this prophecy?

10. What does this parable say about the relationship between morality and entering the kingdom of God?

Day 3 • Read Matthew 21:33–46

THE PARABLE OF THE TENANTS

11. Read Isaiah 5:1–7. What similarities and differences does this passage have to the parable of the tenants?

Similarities Differences

The Coming Judgment
Matthew 21:31–32

Distribute before session 7 for use in session 7.
Use enrichment magazine pp. 19–22.

Resources for Worship

Use these resources for your daily study at home and at the week's assembly.

Hymn

The day is surely drawing near
When Jesus, God's anointed,
In all His power shall appear
As judge whom God appointed.
Then fright shall banish idle mirth,
And flames on flames shall ravage earth
As Scripture long has warned us.

The books are opened then to all,
A record truly telling
What each has done, both great and small,
When he on earth was dwelling,
And ev'ry heart be clearly seen,
And all be known as they have been
In thoughts and words and actions.

My Savior paid the debt I owe
And for my sin was smitten;
Within the Book of Life I know
My name has now been written.
I will not doubt, for I am free,
And Satan cannot threaten me;
There is no condemnation!

May Christ our intercessor be
And through His blood and merit
Read from His book that we are free
With all who life inherit.
Then we shall see Him face to face,
With all His saints in that blest place
Which He has purchased for us.
(*LSB* 508:1, 3, 5, 6)

Prayer

Holy and righteous God, whose judgment is just and whose wrath is severe, grant me to trust in the righteousness of Your Son, Jesus Christ, rather than my own righteousness, that I may escape the wrath to come and celebrate with You in the marriage feast of the Lamb, which has no end, through Jesus Christ, my Lord. Amen.

Digging Deep
My Personal Study for Week 7

Day 1 • Read Luke 16:19–31

THE RICH MAN AND LAZARUS

1. What does the rich man's extravagance in food and dress suggest about him?

2. How might these passages apply in the case of the rich man and Lazarus?

Exodus 23:10–11

Leviticus 19:10

Leviticus 23:22

3. What is the rich man worried about in verses 27–28? What is his proposed solution?

3. Who are the "little ones" referred to in Matthew 18:10?

4. What is the point of the parable? What are we supposed to do?

5. Why is the image of a shepherd seeking his sheep particularly fitting for the point Jesus is making?

Day 2 • Read Matthew 18:21–35

THE PARABLE OF THE UNFORGIVING SERVANT

6. Between yesterday's parable of the lost sheep and today's parable of the unforgiving servant is an interesting and important segue by Jesus (Matthew 18:15–20)—describe it here. What theme does yesterday's parable, the segue, and today's parable share?

7. One talent is the amount of money a laborer would earn for twenty years of steady work. When the king calls the first servant's debt in, the servant promises to repay it (v. 26). How long would it take the servant to pay off his debt?

8. A hundred denarii (duh-NAR-ee, plural of denarius) were the wages for about one third of a year of work. Compared to what the first servant had owed the king, how much did the second servant owe the first one?

9. What is so blameworthy about the first servant's actions? Is forgiveness optional?

10. The king in the parable represents God. What is the meaning of the first servant's massive debt compared to the second servant's small debt?

Living Mercy
Luke 10:36–37

Distribute before session 6 for use in session 6.
Use enrichment magazine pp. 23–25.

Resources for Worship

Use these resources for your daily study at home and at the week's assembly.

Hymn

Lord of glory, You have bought us
With Your lifeblood as the price,
Never grudging for the lost ones
That tremendous sacrifice;
And with that have freely given
Blessings countless as the sand
To the unthankful and the evil
With Your own unsparing hand.

Grant us hearts, dear Lord, to give You
Gladly, freely of Your own.
With the sunshine of Your goodness
Melt our thankless hearts of stone
Till our cold and selfish natures,
Warmed by You, at length believe
That more happy and more blessèd
'Tis to give than to receive.

Wondrous honor You have given
To our humblest charity
In Your own mysterious sentence,
"You have done it all to Me."
Can it be, O gracious Master,
That You deign for alms to sue,
Saying by Your poor and needy,
"Give as I have giv'n to you"?

Lord of glory, You have bought us
With Your lifeblood as the price,
Never grudging for the lost ones
That tremendous sacrifice.
Give us faith to trust You boldly,
Hope, to stay our souls on You;
But, oh, best of all Your graces,
With Your love our love renew.
(*LSB* 851)

Prayer

God of all grace and mercy, who through Your Son, Jesus Christ, has provided me with all I need for this life and the life to come, open my eyes to the needs of the people around me, open my heart to feel compassion toward them, and open my hands to reach out to them in mercy, through Jesus Christ, my Lord. Amen.

Digging Deep
My Personal Study for Week 6

Day 1 • Read Matthew 18:10–14

THE PARABLE OF THE LOST SHEEP

1. This parable sounds much like the parable of the lost sheep in Luke 15:3–7. Write down a few similarities and a few differences between the two parables.

Similarities Differences

2. Read Matthew 18:1–9. Jesus says we must become humble like children to enter the kingdom of God. In what way are children humble? (Be aware that people in Jesus' day would not have seen children as innocent, as we often do today!)

4. a. What does it mean to call God a "rock" in these passages?

Psalm 18:1–6

Psalm 31:1–4

Psalm 62:1–7

b. How might this deepen your understanding of the parable in Matthew 7?

5. When the parable says, "Everyone then who hears these words of Mine and does them," does that mean we are saved by faith plus good works? Why or why not?

Day 2 • Read John 15:1–8

THE VINE AND THE BRANCHES

6. What is the relationship between a branch and its vine (or a branch and the trunk of the tree)? Is the relationship mutual? Explain.

7. Look carefully at verses 2 and 3. Is Jesus talking to believers or unbelievers? What happens to branches that bear no fruit? What happens to branches that do bear fruit?

8. Read Jeremiah 5:1–13. When does the Lord order that branches be removed from His vine?

9. What causes a Christian to stop bearing fruit, according to the parable?

10. Some Christians teach that one cannot fall away from faith if one has truly been saved. How would you respond on the basis of this parable?

Keeping Faith

John 15:5

Distribute before session 5 for use in session 5.
Use enrichment magazine pp. 2–4.

Resources for Worship

Use these resources for your daily study at home and at the week's assembly.

Hymn

My faith looks up to Thee,
Thou Lamb of Calvary,
  Savior divine.
Now hear me while I pray;
Take all my guilt away;
O let me from this day
  Be wholly Thine!

May Thy rich grace impart
Strength to my fainting heart;
  My zeal inspire!
As Thou hast died for me,
Oh, may my love to Thee
Pure, warm, and changeless be,
  A living fire!

While life's dark maze I tread
And griefs around me spread,
  Be Thou my guide;
Bid darkness turn to day,
Wipe sorrow's tears away,
Nor let me ever stray
  From Thee aside.

When ends life's transient dream,
When death's cold, sullen stream
  Shall o'er me roll,
Blest Savior, then, in love,
Fear and distrust remove;
O bear me safe above,
  A ransomed soul!
(*LSB* 702)

Prayer

Lord and Giver of Life, You have called me into Your kingdom through Baptism, and by Your Spirit You sustain me in the one true faith through Word and Sacrament. Use the parables of Jesus to increase my desire to hear Your Word and my fervor to call on You in prayer, through Jesus Christ, my Lord. Amen.

Digging Deep
My Personal Study for Week 5

Day 1 • Read Matthew 7:24–27

THE WISE AND FOOLISH BUILDERS

1. The parable opens in verse 24 with the phrase, "Everyone then who hears these words of Mine." To which "words" is Jesus referring?

2. What warning did Jesus issue just before telling this parable (vv. 21–23)?

3. Read Matthew 16:13–19. What does "rock" mean in that context? Does that meaning for "rock" offer any insight into the parable in Matthew 7?

3. Based on your answer to Question 2, what reasons might the Pharisees have for complaining that Jesus ate with sinners and tax collectors?

4. What does it mean to "receive" someone (v. 2)?

1 Chronicles 12:18

Ezekiel 16:32

Matthew 10:40–41

John 1:11

5. What did it mean that Jesus received sinners, and why did the Pharisees blame Him for it?

Day 2 • Read Luke 15:3–7

THE PARABLE OF THE LOST SHEEP

6. Jesus refers to the Pharisees as shepherds. Read Ezekiel 34:1–10. How would this passage apply to the Pharisees of Jesus' day?

7. Whose fault is it when a sheep gets lost?

8. Shepherds were often hired to care for other people's sheep as well as their own. Would a shepherd freely admit that he had lost one of his sheep? Explain your answer.

9. Why might the shepherd have gathered his friends and neighbors to celebrate finding the sheep? Does the size of the celebration match the occasion?

Lost and Found

Luke 15:7

Distribute before session 4 for use in session 4.
Use enrichment magazine pp. 16–18.

Resources for Worship

Use these resources for your daily study at home and at the week's assembly.

Hymn

Savior, like a shepherd lead us;
  Much we need Your tender care.
In Your pleasant pastures feed us,
  For our use Your fold prepare.
Blessèd Jesus, blessèd Jesus,
  You have bought us; we are Yours.
Blessèd Jesus, blessèd Jesus,
  You have bought us; we are Yours.

We are Yours; in love befriend us,
  Be the guardian of our way;
Keep Your flock, from sin defend us,
  Seek us when we go astray.
Blessèd Jesus, blessèd Jesus,
  Hear us children when we pray.
Blessèd Jesus, blessèd Jesus,
  Hear us children when we pray.

You have promised to receive us,
  Poor and sinful though we be;
You have mercy to relieve us,
  Grace to cleanse, and pow'r to free.
Blessèd Jesus, blessèd Jesus,
  Early let us turn to You.
Blessèd Jesus, blessèd Jesus,
  Early let us turn to You.

Early let us seek Your favor,
  Early let us do Your will;
Blessèd Lord and only Savior,
  With Your love our spirits fill.
Blessèd Jesus, blessèd Jesus,
  You have loved us, love us still.
Blessèd Jesus, blessèd Jesus,
  You have loved us, love us still.
(*LSB* 711)

Prayer

Father of all mercies, You rejoice to give me a place in Your kingdom through the merits of Jesus Christ, my Savior. Open my heart to rejoice with You over every sinner who repents, especially over those whom I might judge to be less worthy of Your kingdom. This I pray through Jesus Christ, my Lord. Amen.

Digging Deep
My Personal Study for Week 4

Day 1 • Read Luke 15:1–2

A LITTLE PHARISEE BACKGROUND

1. Describe the setting for the three parables of Luke 15, such as who was there and what they were saying.

2. Look up the following passages, and then describe what Pharisees believed and how they acted:

Matthew 3:7–10

Matthew 9:9–13

Matthew 12:1–2

Mark 7:1–13

Luke 6:7

4. Who is represented by the sheep in John 10:1–10? Why would someone want to enter the sheep pen without going through the door?

5. Based on your answers to Questions 2–4, what does the sheep pen stand for? Why is Jesus the only way in or out?

Day 2 • Read John 10:11–18

THE GOOD SHEPHERD

6. What did people use sheep for? (For more information, consult a Bible dictionary.)

1 Samuel 25:2

Leviticus 1:10

Deuteronomy 14:4

7. Read Psalm 23. What does the shepherd do, according to the psalm?

8. Read Jeremiah 23:1–6. Who are the shepherds, and what have they done? What does God promise?

9. Read Ezekiel 34:11–16. What does God promise in these verses?

10. How does Jesus fulfill the prophecies from Jeremiah and Ezekiel? What is counterintuitive, or even shocking, about Jesus' statement in John 10:11? (If you need help, look back at Question 6.)

A Most Radical Grace

John 10:11

Distribute before session 3 for use in session 3.
Use enrichment magazine pp. 7–9, 26–28.

Resources for Worship

Use these resources for your daily study at home and at the week's assembly.

Hymn

By grace I'm saved, grace free and boundless;
My soul, believe and doubt it not.
Why stagger at this word of promise?
Has Scripture ever falsehood taught?
No! Then this word must true remain:
By grace you too will life obtain.

By grace! None dare lay claim to merit;
Our works and conduct have no worth.
God in His love sent our Redeemer,
Christ Jesus, to this sinful earth;
His death did for our sins atone,
And we are saved by grace alone.

By grace God's Son, our only Savior,
Came down to earth to bear our sin.
Was it because of your own merit
That Jesus died your soul to win?
No, it was grace, and grace alone,
That brought Him from His heav'nly throne.

By grace! This ground of faith is certain;
As long as God is true, it stands.
What saints have penned by inspiration,
What in His Word our God commands,
Our faith in what our God has done
Depends on grace—grace through His Son.
(*LSB* 566:1–4)

Prayer

Most Holy Father, who gave Your Son, Jesus Christ, as the sacrifice that atones for my sins, send Your Spirit through the parables I study this week to break down my pride and reliance on good works, that I may instead humbly receive the perfect righteousness of Your Son, through whom I pray. Amen.

Digging Deep
My Personal Study for Week 3

Day 1 • Read John 10:1–18

THE GOOD SHEPHERD

1. How many different images does Jesus use to describe Himself in this passage? What are the images? In which verse(s) does He change from one image to another?

2. Focus on the first image for Questions 2–4. Read verse 7 again. In light of that verse, what does Jesus mean by not using the door of the sheep pen but instead climbing in by some other way (v. 1)?

3. Skim John 9, reading verses 35–41 closely. What is the context for the first parable in John 10?

4. Why would God scatter the seed of His Word like a reckless farmer?

Day 2 • Read Mark 1:40–2:17

HEALING AND FASTING

5. Mark 1:40–45 is about a man who has an infectious skin disease. If you were seriously ill and met Jesus, what would you ask for? What is surprising about the man's request? Read Leviticus 13:45–46 and 7:19–21. Why would the man specifically ask to be cleansed rather than healed?

6. Read Leviticus 14:1–9. What was the priests' role in the healing of leprosy? What did Jesus do for the man? How does He compare to the priests?

7. Why do the scribes complain in Mark 2:6–7? How does Jesus respond? What is the point?

8. Levi is better known as Matthew. What was his occupation? If you have time, look up his occupation in a Bible dictionary and describe how Jews viewed that occupation, and why.

9. What complaint did the scribes voice against Jesus after He ate at Levi's house? What does their complaint tell us about their understanding of salvation?

Day 3 • Read Matthew 9:14–15

THE WEDDING GUESTS

10. What question introduces the first parable?

11. If you have time, look up fasting in a Bible dictionary and describe how people in Jesus' day understood it. You might also look at Matthew 6:16–18.

Something Old, Something New

Matthew 9:15–17

Distribute before session 2 for use in session 2.
Use enrichment magazine pp. 29–32.

Resources for Worship

Use these resources for your daily study at home and at the week's assembly.

Hymn

Almighty God, Your Word is cast
Like seed into the ground;
Now let the dew of heav'n descend
And righteous fruits abound.

Let not the sly satanic foe
This holy seed remove,
But give it root in ev'ry heart
To bring forth fruits of love.

Let not the world's deceitful cares
The rising plant destroy,
But let it yield a hundredfold
The fruits of peace and joy.

So when the precious seed is sown,
Life-giving grace bestow
That all whose souls the truth receive
Its saving pow'r may know.
(*LSB* 577)

Prayer

Good and gracious Father, whose Son shows us the true meaning of the Old Testament in the forgiveness He won for us on the cross, use the parables I study in the coming weeks to plant the seed of Your Word in my heart, that I may attain life everlasting, through Jesus Christ, my Lord. Amen.

Digging Deep
My Personal Study for Week 2

Day 1 • Read Matthew 13:3–9, 18–23

THE PARABLE OF THE SOWER

1. Many farmers till the ground or use no-till planters that bury the seed beneath the surface of the ground. They also choose ground suitable for the crops they are planting. With this in mind, what might be surprising about the farmer's actions in the parable? Do you believe this is how most farmers in Jesus' day sowed their seed?

2. What does the seed in the parable represent? Who, then, does the sower stand for? What point is Jesus making?

3. Read Isaiah 55:1–11. Why does God send out His Word, and what is its purpose?

4. **Challenge question.** Why would God be so intent on pouring out His wrath against the Israelites in Isaiah's day?

5. How does the passage from Isaiah help to explain the troubling words of Jesus in Matthew 13:10–17? Why does Jesus obscure the message of salvation by telling parables?

Day 2 • Read Matthew 13:34–35

THE PURPOSE OF PARABLES

6. According to these two verses, why does Jesus speak in parables?

7. Read Psalm 78:1–4, which is quoted in these two verses of Matthew. What does the psalmist reveal, to whom, and why?

8. Parables are meant not only to obscure but also to reveal the truth of God's salvation. What indications of this do you see in yesterday's reading, Matthew 13:10–17?

9. Read Colossians 1:24–29. What is the mystery that has been revealed in these last times?

Day 3 • Read Matthew 13:31–33

THE PARABLES OF THE MUSTARD SEED AND THE LEAVEN

10. How does leaven work in a batch of dough? Can you see it at work? What does that say about the kingdom of heaven?

11. Read Matthew 18:20. What encouragement does this passage and the parable of the leaven give to Christian congregations (especially small ones)?

Why Parables?

Matthew 13:34–35

Distribute before session 1 for use in session 1.
Use enrichment magazine pp. 5–6, 16–18.

Resources for Worship

Use these resources for your daily study at home and at the week's assembly.

Hymn

Speak, O Lord, Your servant listens,
Let Your Word to me come near;
Newborn life and spirit give me,
Let each promise still my fear.
Death's dread pow'r, its inward strife,
Wars against Your Word of life;
Fill me, Lord, with love's strong fervor
That I cling to You forever!

Oh, what blessing to be near You
And to listen to Your voice;
Let me ever love and hear You,
Let Your Word be now my choice!
Many hardened sinners, Lord,
Flee in terror at Your Word;
But to all who feel sin's burden
You give words of peace and pardon.

Lord, Your words are waters living
When my thirsting spirit pleads.
Lord, Your words are bread life-giving;
On Your words my spirit feeds.
Lord, Your words will be my light
Through death's cold and dreary night;
Yes, they are my sword prevailing
And my cup of joy unfailing!

As I pray, dear Jesus, hear me;
Let Your words in me take root.
May Your Spirit e'er be near me
That I bear abundant fruit.
May I daily sing Your praise,
From my heart glad anthems raise,
Till my highest praise is given
In the endless joy of heaven.
(*LSB* 589)

Prayer

Merciful heavenly Father, whose Son entered this world as an infant and slept in a manger, open my eyes to the mighty work You do through means such as Your Word and Sacraments, and help me to trust that You are at work for my salvation even when I cannot see it, through Your Son, Jesus Christ, our Lord. Amen.

Digging Deep
My Personal Study for Week 1

Day 1 • Read Matthew 13:10–17

THE PURPOSE OF PARABLES

1. This passage is among the more difficult in the Scriptures. Why, according to Jesus, does He speak in parables?

2. Read Isaiah 6. This is the passage that Jesus quotes when He explains why He preaches in parables. What is the setting? Why does Isaiah say, "Woe is me"?

3. Read Isaiah 5:1–7. Why would God tell Isaiah, "Make the heart of this people dull" (6:10)? What have they done to deserve such treatment? Have they had any chances to repent?

Study Guide

The Parable of the Two Sons, Leslie Benson/ © Concordia Publishing House

Sometimes, one topic leads to another, and a collection of sayings develops a theme. These, then, become the *sermons* of Jesus. They are especially characteristic of the evangelist Matthew, who preserved a number of them. A good example is our Lord's discourse on the end times in Matthew 24–25.

The evangelists also record *dialogues* that our Lord engaged in with His disciples or opponents. Although most of the talking in these passages is done by Jesus, they retain a conversational character. John reports several of them, such as Jesus' talking with the woman at the well (John 4:7–26) or His dispute with the Jewish leaders that led to their almost stoning Him (John 8:12–59).

Besides the words of Jesus, the evangelists also record His deeds, and in many instances it is impossible really to separate the two. Nevertheless, when action rather than conversation predominates, we classify such passages as *narratives*. They constitute major portions of the Gospels. We could recall, for example, the Passion and Resurrection narratives. The words of Jesus remain important in these contexts, but His deeds—suffering, dying, and rising again—have their own special and redemptive purposes. Likewise, the nativity, infancy, and childhood stories at the beginning of Matthew and Luke are also uniquely significant. The coming of Jesus, the "God with us" (Matthew 1:23), marks the turning point of human history even before He utters a word.

Elsewhere in the Gospels, there are stories that fall into several subtypes of narrative, some that call attention to Jesus' words, others that describe His role as promised Messiah, and, of course, His miracles. The *miracle stories* themselves can be organized into additional subtypes; for example, healings, casting out demons, and raising the dead. There are also nature miracles, such as the feeding of the five thousand (Matthew 14:15–21) and calming a storm (Matthew 8:23–27). In each of the miracle stories, our Lord addresses a dire human situation with supernatural power. Altogether Jesus' miracles are impressive demonstrations of His divine nature *and* of His compassion, since He uses His power to relieve the sufferings of men.

Besides the miracle stories, there are other stories that reveal Jesus as God's special representative. Sometimes Jesus' words or deeds evoke a kind of amazed recognition from those who are present. Already in Mark 1, the evangelist records such a reaction from those who hear Jesus teach (vv. 35–39) and then from the same people when they see Him heal (vv. 40–45). In other cases, someone clearly confesses that Jesus is the Messiah. Think, for example, of Peter's confession (Matthew 16:16). In still others, Jesus acts in a way that shows His authority. The *calling stories* are good examples of this type, for in these episodes, Jesus summons someone into discipleship, and the person obeys at once, as in the calling of Matthew (Matthew 9:9).

Of course, not everyone who hears Jesus follows Him, so *conflict stories* are another common subtype in the Gospels. In these accounts, Jesus confronts His enemies directly. In fact, Jesus also aims some of His sayings right at His foes. In Matthew 23, the evangelist has preserved an entire discourse that pronounces judgment upon the scribes and Pharisees.

These religious leaders, along with the chief priests, often criticize and question our Lord. Such episodes occur early (Mark 2:7) and late (Mark 12:34) in Jesus' ministry. Sometimes, they involve a single critic, as with Simon the Pharisee (Luke 7:36–50); other times, an entire group, such as the Sadducees (Luke 20:27–40). These encounters can be deliberate, such as the Pharisees' question about paying taxes (Matthew 22:15–22), but other times they seem spontaneous, as when the disciples plucked grain on the Sabbath (Matthew 12:1–8). In every instance, our Lord demonstrates His mastery of the situation.

Sometimes, a conflict culminates in a striking and memorable saying of Jesus, such as "Render to Caesar the things that are Caesar's, and to God the things that are God's" (Matthew 22:21). Stories that conclude in a noteworthy statement like this are *pronouncement stories*. They do not have to be conflicts. The Zacchaeus story (Luke 19:1–10) is another good example. It concludes with a beautiful Gospel saying, "The Son of Man came to seek and to save the lost."

The Final Point

Literary analysis of the type we are discussing here involves identifying the various elements that each evangelist uses to present the story of Jesus. But its only purpose is to assist in our understanding of the Gospels.

We are doing a disservice to any author if, by analyzing the parts, we miss the significance of the whole. In the case of the Gospels, this would be especially unfortunate. We are not dealing with fiction but with fact, not with the work of men but of God. In our Lord Jesus Christ, God has acted decisively in time and space to obtain salvation for all. *That's* the one element of Gospel analysis that we must never omit.

A DENARIUS A DAY

"After agreeing with the laborers for a denarius a day, he sent them into his vineyard" (Matthew 20:2). Thankfully, most Bibles today have footnotes. How else would we know how much these workers were being paid? And, incidentally, what were workers supposed to do in a vineyard? And why did they grow grapes in the first place? For jelly or for wine?

The parables of our Lord are filled with details from everyday life that raise all sorts of questions for modern readers. What we have in common with the first readers is that we still have to make a living, but what's different is how—and oh, yes, for how much?

Making Money

Let's deal first of all with the money. Bible translators wrestle with how to handle the biblical terms for money. On the one hand, if they use modern terminology like dollars or Euros, they subtly shift the scene from ancient Palestine to modern America or Europe. They also run the risk of their translation's soon becoming obsolete on account of changing values in modern currencies because of inflation.

On the other hand, if translators retain the words from the original language, the ordinary reader won't understand. To complicate matters even further, the New Testament was written in Greek, but the common money was often Roman. Thus, the English Standard Version uses the Latin word *denarius* for the Greek word *denerion* in Matthew 20:2, 9–10, 13; but it translates the Greek word *drachma* as "coin" in Luke 15:8–9. Since neither translation informs the reader of what either monetary unit was worth, the ESV editors have added a note to explain that a denarius and a drachma both represented the normal day's wage for a worker. Of course, that still leaves us wondering what a denarius (or drachma) could actually buy, but at least we have some idea of a person's situation if he earned one.

But how did people earn their *denarii* in the first place? Because the biblical narratives took place long before the industrial revolution, most people worked very hard physically in jobs that were closely connected to nature. In the parables, for example, Jesus told stories about fishing, farming, and growing grapes.

Fishing was the livelihood of the first disciples Jesus called (Mark 1:16–20); they plied their trade on the Sea of Galilee. Two of them, brothers James and John, worked for their father, Zebedee. A family business made a lot of sense, since the capital outlay for boats and nets was substantial and the work required more than one pair of hands. Although on one occasion Jesus directed Peter to catch a fish by means of hook and line (Matthew 17:27), the more typical way was by means of a dragnet. Fishermen would arrange a large net in a circle in the water and then draw it in gradually to their boat at the center, or they would arrange the net in a semicircle and then pull it in to the shore. With the dragnet, one was likely to catch many things besides edible fish that would have to be discarded or cast back into the sea (see Matthew 13:47–48).

Farming was the occupation of many more people than was fishing. The fertile farmlands and orchards were familiar territory to Jesus, and He included many references to agriculture in His parables and sayings. Among the farming tasks mentioned in the Gospels are plowing (Luke 9:62), which began the agricultural season after the rains of autumn; planting seed (Matthew 13:3); fertilizing with manure (Luke 13:8); harvesting (Matthew 9:37–38); reaping by means of a sickle (Mark 4:29); binding weeds into bundles for burning (Matthew 13:30); threshing and winnowing or sifting to separate grain from chaff (Matthew 3:12; Luke 22:31); and storing grain in barns (Matthew 3:12).

Farmers cultivated numerous crops in Israel. The Gospels mention wheat eight times, but in Deuteronomy 8:8, Moses described the Promised Land as "a land of wheat and barley, of vines and fig trees and pomegranates, a land of olive trees and honey." In Joshua 2:6, there is a reference to flax, and in Ezekiel 4:9, the prophet spoke of wheat, barley, beans, lentils, millet, and emmer (a type of wheat). Very prominent in the Scriptures is also the growing of grapes.

Grapes had many uses in biblical times. They were eaten as fruit, dried into raisins, and turned into jelly by boiling down the juice, but most of the crop went into making wine. Beginning a vineyard was hard work. The land itself had to be cultivated before planting and then surrounded by a ditch or a wall as protection from predators. Within the vineyard, the owner would also construct a tower to watch for adversaries (animal or human) and, of course, a winepress, a tank made out of stone in which workers would crush the grapes and then retrieve the juice, which was then stored it in either clay pots or goatskin bags. The latter were ideal for juice that was fermenting into wine (see Matthew 9:17).

Growing and harvesting grapes was labor intensive. Owners routinely would hire day laborers as the work and time of year demanded (the growing season was approximately from spring to fall). Sometimes, owners would lease the vineyard to others and take part of the harvest as rent. Our Lord referred to both arrangements in His parables (see Matthew 20:1–16; 21:33–40).

In the parable of the two sons (Matthew 21:28–32), the father sent his sons to "work in the vineyard." Jesus also referred to grape-growing in Luke 6:44 ("nor are grapes picked from a bramble bush"), and especially in John 15:1–8 ("I am the true vine, and My Father is the vinedresser . . ."). So clearly, Jesus expected His hearers to be familiar with the cultivation of grapes.

And also with wine. Our Lord's first miracle was turning water into wine (John 2:1–12), and His enemies called Him "a glutton and drunkard [literally, *wine-drinker*]" (Matthew 11:19). But Jesus also referred to drinking "the fruit of the vine" in connection with the arrival of God's kingdom (Luke 22:18) and, of course, He used wine when He instituted Holy Communion.

Eating and Drinking for Eternity

One of the tragedies of our human nature is that we take God's good gifts and turn them into sin, so the Bible includes many warnings. For example, there are warnings against the misuse of money ("The love of money is a root of all kinds of evils"; 1 Timothy 6:10) as well as excessive eating and drinking ("The drunkard and the glutton will come to poverty, and slumber will clothe them with rags"; Proverbs 23:21).

How amazing it is, therefore, that God actually *uses* food and drink to bring us eternal blessings. In Holy Communion, our Lord offers His true body and blood for us Christians to eat and to drink—"given and shed for you for the forgiveness of sins." And for that, we don't need a footnote!

Samaria *and* Samaritans

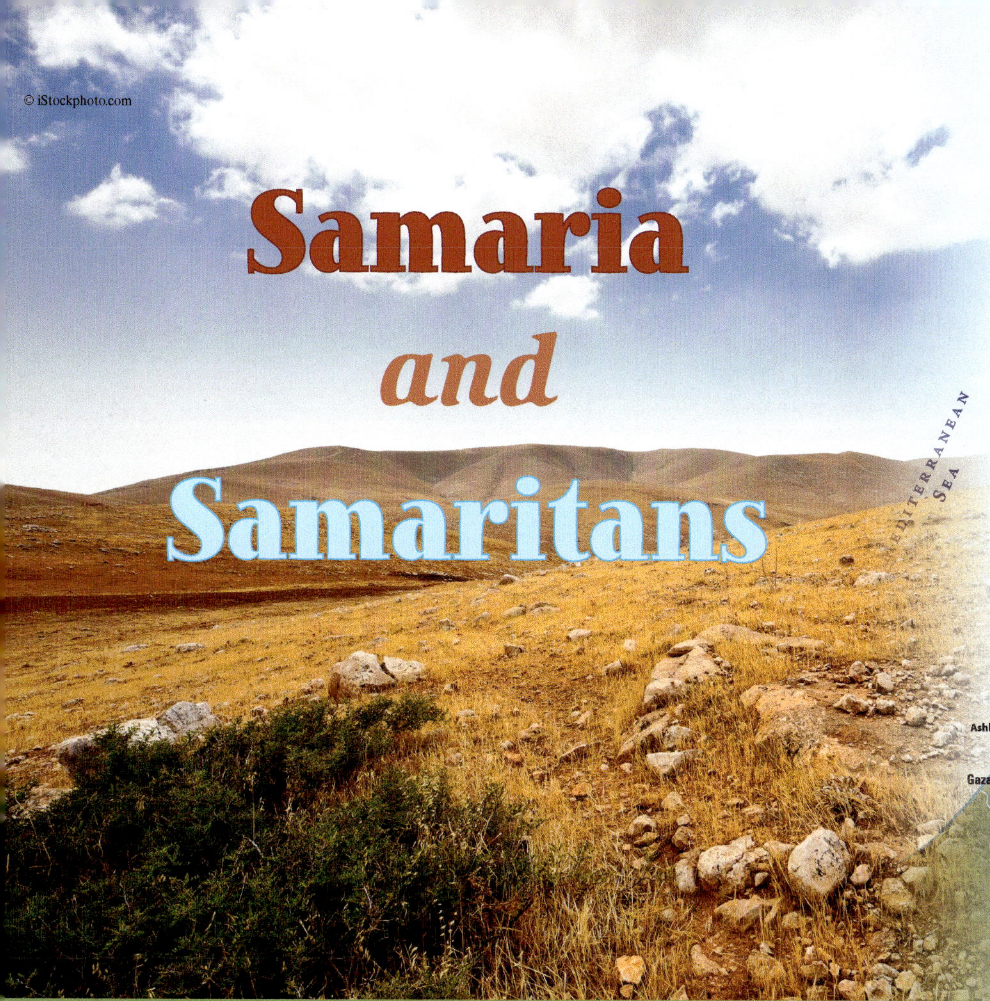

Map from *The Lutheran Study Bible*/© CPH

If you look at a map of the Holy Land from the time of Jesus, ʼou will see Samaria nestled between Judea in the south and Galilee in the north. Unlike those other two regions, however, ›amaria was not often visited by our Lord. In fact, the evangelist ohn reported that "Jews have no dealings with Samaritans" (John :.9). So any interaction with them by Jesus and His disciples was xceptional.

But why was that? Just who were the Samaritans, and what ʌas the origin of their territory and religion? They had a lot in ommon with the Jews besides sharing a neighborhood, but not nough to keep them from becoming enemies.

Beginnings

The origins of the Samaritans began many centuries before Christ, especially during the time when Israel was divided into two kingdoms, north and south, following the death of Solomon (931 BC). Although the Northern Kingdom included ten of the twelve tribes and was often more prosperous and powerful than the Southern Kingdom, the latter retained the temple and priesthood, as well as the Davidic line of kings. In the north, Jeroboam, the first of the kings after the division, introduced new places of worship outside of Jerusalem and new forms of worship, including golden calves (1 Kings 12:26–33). Right from the beginning, therefore, religion in the north combined elements from paganism with the true worship of God.

© iStockphoto.com

The situation became even worse some sixty years later, when King Ahab and his wife Jezebel promoted Baal worship in Israel. This was a particularly hideous form of idolatry that sometimes included human sacrifice (Jeremiah 19:4–5). However, even though idolatry was widespread in the north, there were also those who remained faithful to the Lord. For God raised up prophets such as Elijah and Elisha to rebuke the powerful for their sins, and He preserved a remnant of those who neither bowed to Baal nor kissed him (1 Kings 19:18). Other prophets God raised up to preach to the Northern Kingdom were Jonah, Amos, and Hosea.

The cult of Baal included multiple shrines and images, and Ahab's devotion resulted in a temple for his false god right in the new capital city of the north, Samaria. Ahab's father, Omri, had succeeded to the throne after civil war and was one of Israel's most impressive kings, but he did not retreat at all from the idolatry of his predecessors. He did, however, build a new capital, named Samaria after Shemer, the original owner of its location, on a hill overlooking the principal north-south travel route through the country (1 Kings 16:24). Under Omri, Samaria and its people prospered greatly. The name of the city was also used for the entire region (1 Kings 13:32; Ezra 4:10).

In spite of the blessings that the Northern Kingdom enjoyed, its wickedness and idolatry were so great that God finally determined to destroy it (2 Kings 17:7–18). His agents for this punishment were the Assyrians, a fierce and idolatrous people themselves. God had already destroyed the family of Ahab and the temple of Baal in Samaria through Jehu, who then took the throne (2 Kings 10:27), but neither Jehu nor his successors returned to the pure worship of God, in spite of God's pleas through the prophets. So the Lord turned the Assyrians loose upon Israel. In 722 BC, the city of Samaria fell and the Northern Kingdom ceased to be an independent state.

A Turning Point

As a part of their ravaging of the Northern Kingdom, the Assyrians hauled off into exile thousands of Israelites and replaced them with people from other places. The Bible first used the term "Samaritan" for these newcomers (2 Kings 17:29). Over the decades that followed, these people developed their own culture *and* religion. On the one hand, the Samaritan religion included elements from the true worship of the Lord. On the other hand, it was pervaded by practices and deities derived from the paganism they had brought with them into

© Renata Sedmakova/Shuttterstock, Inc.

Israel (2 Kings 17:24–41). The result was syncretism—a mixture of religions—instead of worship of the one true God, which He Himself had prescribed to Israel of old.

On one occasion, the Samaritans sought to identify their faith with that of the Jews, who were called such on account of belonging to the tribe of Judah, which inhabited the Southern Kingdom. The Jews had escaped destruction at the hands of the Assyrians in the eighth century BC only to be taken into captivity by the Babylonians in the sixth. However, God preserved them as a distinct people, continued to send them prophets, and then permitted them to return from exile, to restore Jerusalem, and to rebuild the temple.

And the Samaritans wanted to help. They even claimed that they worshiped the same God and made sacrifices to Him; but the Jewish leaders refused, since their duty was to retain God's revealed religion in its truth and purity (Ezra 4:1–3). Thus, Jews and Samaritans inhabited neighboring territories but were two different peoples who practiced two different faiths.

Interestingly, the Samaritans did share a Bible with the Jews—at least, part of it, the Pentateuch. But they had their own version. They also accepted the Sabbath, circumcision, and the sacred feasts, and they looked forward to a Messiah. But they rejected the claims of Jerusalem and its temple. The Samaritans built their own temple (destroyed by the Maccabean dynasty of the Jews, c. 128 BC) on their own "holy" mount, Gerizim (near the ancient city of Shechem). In their "Bible," they named this mountain the site of Old Testament episodes such as the sacrifice of Isaac. The significance of Mount Gerizim, therefore, became a focal point of the conflict between Samaritans and Jews.

Samaritans and the Gospel

At the time of Jesus, hostility between the two groups was as intense as ever. On one occasion, when our Lord sought to enter a Samaritan village but was refused, His disciples suggested calling down fire from heaven to destroy it (Luke 9:52–54)! How surprising it must have been, therefore, when Jesus healed a Samaritan leper (Luke 17:12–19) or used a Samaritan to exemplify neighborly love in a parable (Luke 10:29–37). And how shocking it must have been when Jesus requested a drink of water from a Samaritan woman and then, through her, brought the Gospel to an entire Samaritan village (John 4:1–42).

Jesus' last words to His disciples at the time of His ascension included a commission to witness for Him in Samaria (Acts 1:8). In spite of all the idolatry that had characterized this land and the false religion that the people still practiced, God's Word was for them. This was good news for the Samaritans, as it is also for us—God's grace is for everyone.

© Shuttterstock, Inc.

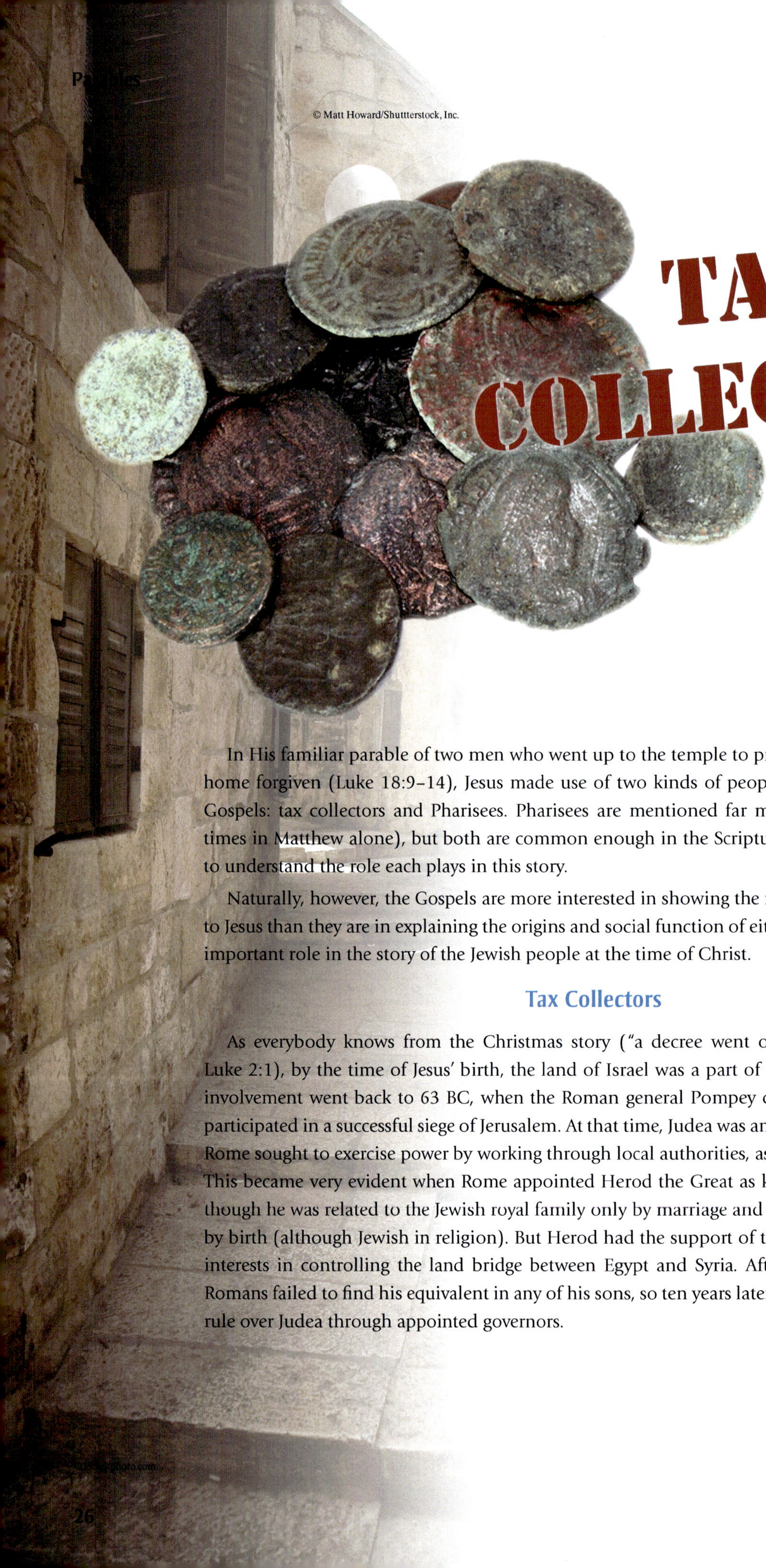

TAX COLLECTORS

In His familiar parable of two men who went up to the temple to pray while only one returned home forgiven (Luke 18:9–14), Jesus made use of two kinds of people who often appear in the Gospels: tax collectors and Pharisees. Pharisees are mentioned far more frequently (over thirty times in Matthew alone), but both are common enough in the Scriptures for a Bible reader easily to understand the role each plays in this story.

Naturally, however, the Gospels are more interested in showing the relationship of these groups to Jesus than they are in explaining the origins and social function of either one. But each played an important role in the story of the Jewish people at the time of Christ.

Tax Collectors

As everybody knows from the Christmas story ("a decree went out from Caesar Augustus"; Luke 2:1), by the time of Jesus' birth, the land of Israel was a part of the Roman Empire. Roman involvement went back to 63 BC, when the Roman general Pompey campaigned in the east and participated in a successful siege of Jerusalem. At that time, Judea was an independent kingdom and Rome sought to exercise power by working through local authorities, as was typical of the Romans. This became very evident when Rome appointed Herod the Great as king of Judea (37 BC), even though he was related to the Jewish royal family only by marriage and was in fact Arab (Idumean) by birth (although Jewish in religion). But Herod had the support of the Romans and suited their interests in controlling the land bridge between Egypt and Syria. After Herod died (1 BC), the Romans failed to find his equivalent in any of his sons, so ten years later Rome was exercising direct rule over Judea through appointed governors.

AND PHARISEES

Naturally enough, the Romans expected their territories to pay, and among the taxes imposed in Judea was a customs tax; in other words, a tax on goods as they moved from one place to another. In order to secure a reliable income, the Romans sold the right to collect the tax in any particular district. The purchaser, in turn, hired others to do the actual collecting and placed them at commercially strategic places, where they could extract money from merchants by means of Roman authority—and force, if necessary.

Nobody likes to pay taxes, of course. But the Jews especially resented having to pay a Roman tax. Moreover, the tax collectors were notorious for exploiting the system and virtually extorting money from taxpayers in order to cover their payments to the Romans and still make a generous profit for themselves. Tax collectors, therefore, were reckoned as thieves and traitors in first-century Israel. No wonder, then, that the evangelists grouped them with other public "sinners" (e.g., Mark 2:16).

It was extraordinary, therefore, that our Lord associated with tax collectors, but He did. He had come also for them. Two tax collectors are named in the Gospels: Zacchaeus, "a chief tax collector" (perhaps supervisor of collections in Jericho; Luke 19:2), and Matthew (also known as Levi), whom Jesus called to be an apostle (Matthew 9:9; Mark 2:14).

Pharisees

At the opposite extreme from tax collectors in Jewish society were the Pharisees. Jesus also associated with them, but they were some of His worst critics and foes. They had position and prominence, yet they perceived Jesus as a threat. But why?

To understand the Pharisees' opposition to Jesus, it helps to know their background. The Pharisees were a religious/political faction whose origins could be traced back to the Time between the Testaments, when Judea was ruled by the Hasmoneans. This dynasty had come to power as a result of a successful revolt by the Jews against the Seleucid monarchs of Syria. The rebellion began when King Antiochus Epiphanes (d. 164 BC) ordered harsh measures against the Jewish religion and even went so far as to desecrate the temple by authorizing sacrifices to Zeus. Many Jews yielded, but others did not, inspired by the defiance of a priest named Matthias and his five sons, known as the "Maccabees," from the Hebrew word for "hammer."

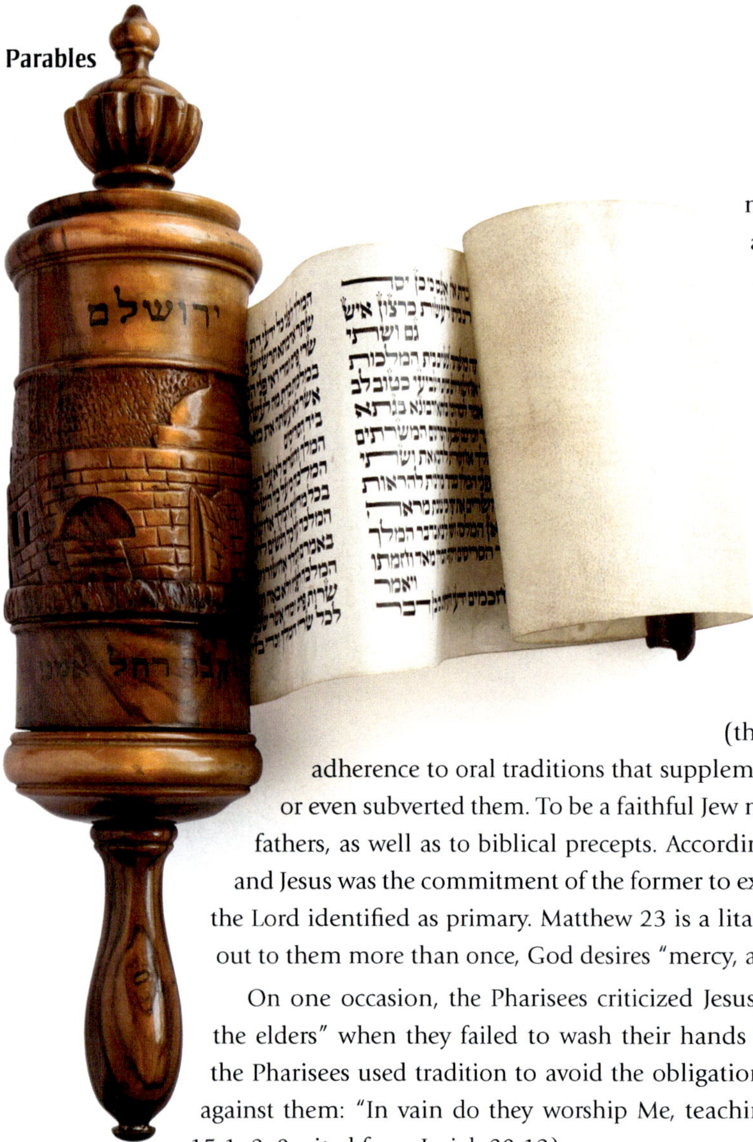

While the Maccabees (or Hasmoneans, their dynastic name) were leading the fight to throw off Syrian rule, they also established themselves at the head of Jewish society. In fact, they ended up ruling Judea until the coming of the Romans as both kings and high priests. But this development was distressing to some of the Jewish people who knew that God had established the latter in the family of Aaron and the former in the family of David. Therefore, in the second century BC, a faction or party emerged that opposed the Hasmonean intrusion into divinely appointed offices that did not belong to them. These were the Pharisees.

Besides their rejection of the Hasmonean claims, the Pharisees identified true religion with devotion to the Law, but not just the written Law of God (the Torah, or Pentateuch). The Pharisees also advocated adherence to oral traditions that supplemented and developed the principles of the written Law—or even subverted them. To be a faithful Jew meant to be scrupulously adherent to the traditions of the fathers, as well as to biblical precepts. Accordingly, a frequent source of conflict between the Pharisees and Jesus was the commitment of the former to external observances at the expense of neighborly love that the Lord identified as primary. Matthew 23 is a litany of Jesus' charges against the Pharisees. As He pointed out to them more than once, God desires "mercy, and not sacrifice" (Matthew 9:13; 12:7).

On one occasion, the Pharisees criticized Jesus for permitting His disciples to "break the tradition of the elders" when they failed to wash their hands before eating. The Lord's answer was to point out that the Pharisees used tradition to avoid the obligations of the Fourth Commandment, and He quoted Isaiah against them: "In vain do they worship Me, teaching as doctrines the commandments of men" (Matthew 15:1–2, 9; cited from Isaiah 29:13).

Everybody's Savior

Given the ongoing hostility of the Pharisees toward Jesus during His ministry, it is no surprise to find them at the forefront of the coalition that sought His death (John 11:47–53). Faith in Christ demands repentance, and repentance is premised on the recognition of sin. Pharisees could see sin in tax collectors, but they had trouble seeing it in themselves (Luke 18:11).

But that's not the end of the story, for God was gracious also to Pharisees. Nicodemus was a Pharisee, and he assisted in the burial of Jesus. Then, after Pentecost, Pharisees began to believe. But, of course, the most famous of these, "a Pharisee, a son of Pharisees" (Acts 23:6), was none other than Paul, the greatest of the apostles. For our Lord died for all sins and sinners, tax collectors and Pharisees too.

WORD Pictures

God has chosen to reveal Himself by words—the words of the Bible. But words come in different forms. Legal language, for example, is direct and unambiguous. It appeals to the intellect. Mathematical and scientific languages are similar.

But other forms of language involve the imagination as well as the intellect. They communicate by creating mental pictures as well as by stating propositions. Communication like this is often more effective than the plainer types, for it engages a person more thoroughly, affectively as well as intellectually. People like what they hear (or read) and are also able to understand it.

The second type of communication is far more characteristic of the Bible than the first. From the beginning of the Scriptures until the end, God uses word pictures to convey His truth.

Similes and Metaphors

Everyone loves Psalm 23. But why? On account of its message that God cares for us? That's part of it, for sure. Especially when we are frightened or sad, the truth that God cares is all important—comforting and reassuring. But there is more to the Twenty-third Psalm than its message. We also enjoy the images through which God has conveyed His comfort: a shepherd leading his sheep to good grazing and then standing watch with rod and staff as they pass through the dark valley; a luxurious banquet set in the middle of enemies; and finally, abiding in God's house forever. Through such pictures, the Scriptures encourage us to feel the comfort that God promises. To put it another way, language like this moves us to experience what it is that the Bible affirms.

Perhaps the most basic of word pictures is the *simile*. It is an explicit comparison—using words such as "like" or "as"—between things not usually compared. If I say, "John looks like his brother," that is simply a comparison, but if I say, "John looks like a freight train when he plays football," that is a simile. The teaching of Jesus is full of similes. In Matthew 10:16, for example, Jesus used three of them in a single verse, "Behold, I am sending you out *as sheep in the midst of wolves*, so be *wise as serpents* and *innocent as doves*." Parables are sometimes thought of as extended similes because Jesus began so many of them with the words "The kingdom of heaven is *like* . . ."

Closely related to a simile is the *metaphor*. This is an implied comparison; that is, without the "like" or "as." "John is a freight train when he plays football" is an example of a metaphor. Metaphors are bolder than similes in that they say what something really *is* rather than merely what something is *like*. But the actual meaning of the two figures may be the same. In both statements about John and the freight train, the speaker is describing John's athletic style, but the metaphor says it in a heightened or more emphatic manner.

Frequently, our Lord used metaphors in addition to similes. The Sermon on the Mount has a lot of them, such as "you are the salt of the earth" (Matthew 5:13); "you are the light of the world" (5:14); "when you give to the needy, sound no trumpet before you" (6:2); "the speck that is in your brother's eye" (7:3); "do not throw your pearls before pigs" (7:6); "knock, and it will be opened" (7:7); and "enter by the narrow gate" (7:13).

Both metaphors and similes make demands on us hearers (or readers). First, we have to use our imagination. We have to picture in our mind the object of comparison in order to discover the point of comparison. This means, secondly, that we must be familiar with the objects referred to by the speaker—whether freight trains or doves or narrow gates. Otherwise, these figures do not communicate effectively. Finally, we have to interpret the phrase. We have to locate the intended point of comparison, because the subject and object are not the same. Sometimes, the point is explicit, as in "wise as serpents," but other times it is not, as in "sheep in the midst of wolves." In the latter case, we have to figure out for ourself that this is a picture of danger. All of these—imagination, familiarity, and interpretation—require mental activity, but that activity involves us by pulling us into the text.

Perhaps the most familiar of our Lord's metaphors is a series of "I am" statements recorded in the Gospel of John. The evangelist recorded twenty-two statements (based on the original Greek) in which Jesus said, "I am . . ." Many of these passages are not metaphors (e.g., "Jesus said to them, 'I am He'"; 18:5), but several of them are. They are word pictures by which our Lord revealed His nature and work by identifying Himself with common objects such as bread, light, and shepherds.

Jesus said, "I am the bread of life" (John 6:35). On the one hand, His point was to teach the people that ordinary bread, or even extraordinary bread, such as manna in the wilderness, sustains life here and now but keeps no one from dying. On the other hand, only Jesus—and faith in Him—brings a life that never ends.

But for whom does Jesus provide eternal life? He offers it to everyone. Jesus said, "I am the light of the world," and then He explained, "Whoever follows Me will not walk in darkness, but will have the light of life" (John 8:12). In the next chapter, Jesus performed a miracle that illustrated His metaphor. He healed the man born blind *and* revealed Himself as the Savior (9:35–38).

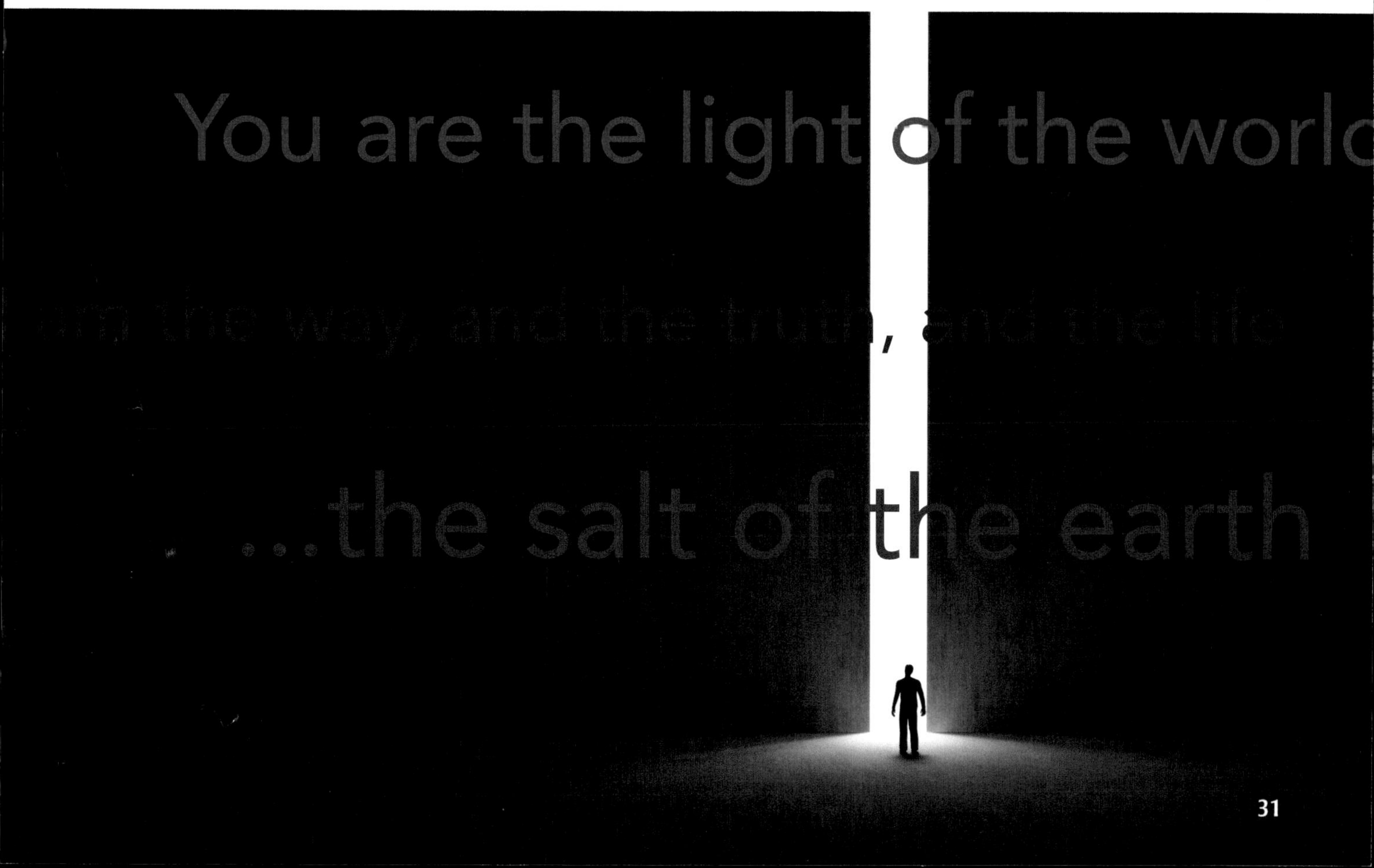

Jesus also called Himself "the good shepherd" (John 10:11, 14). Once again, He explained His own metaphor. The *good* shepherd protects His sheep even to the point of death; the *good* shepherd knows His sheep and they know Him. In this word picture, our Lord depicted the character and purpose of His own death: in obedience to the Father, on behalf of His people, that they might have life.

Why Analyze?

By analyzing the similes and metaphors in the words of Jesus, we come to appreciate the artistry and skill that our Lord employed when teaching. Jesus' sayings, sermons, and parables appeal to our imagination and encourage us to experience the truths that they convey. Thus, the Word made flesh (John 1:14) communicated the Word of God very effectively in the words of men.

But rhetorical analysis of Jesus' teaching is not an end in itself. Neither is historical analysis that investigates the past as recorded in the Scriptures, nor even theological analysis that presents God's truth in doctrinal form. No, instead, biblical analysis of any kind achieves its true goal only when it helps us to hear and keep the Word of God.